Protests in the Streets

1968 Across the Globe

Series Editor: Alfred J. Andrea
Emeritus Professor of History
University of Vermont

Protests in the Streets

1968 Across the Globe

Elaine Carey

Hackett Publishing Company, Inc.
Indianapolis/Cambridge

19 18 17 16   1 2 3 4 5 6 7

For further information, please address
  Hackett Publishing Company, Inc.
  P.O. Box 44937
  Indianapolis, Indiana 46244-0937

  www.hackettpublishing.com

Cover design by Rick Todhunter
Interior design by Elizabeth L. Wilson
Composition by Aptara, Inc.

Library of Congress Cataloging-in-Publication Data

Names: Carey, Elaine, 1967– author.
Title: Protests in the streets : 1968 across the globe / Elaine Carey.
Other titles: 1968 across the globe
Description: Indianapolis : Hackett Publishing Company, Inc., [2016] | Series:
  Critical themes in world history | Includes index.
Identifiers: LCCN 2016009482 | ISBN 9781624665264 (pbk.) |
  ISBN 9781624665271 (cloth)
Subjects: LCSH: Nineteen sixty-eight, A.D. | Protest movements—History—
  20th century. | Student movements—History—20th century. |
  Radicalism—History—20th century. | Government, Resistance to—
  History—20th century. | World politics—1965–1975.
Classification: LCC D848 .C36 2016 | DDC 909.82/6—dc23
LC record available at http://lccn.loc.gov/2016009482

CONTENTS

SERIES EDITOR'S FOREWORD

History never repeats itself. Circumstances are never the same, and human agency, chance, and accident play key roles in the unfolding of events. That noted, it is tempting, as Elaine Carey, the lead author of this book, points out in the epilogue, "The Streets Speak, 1968 and Today," to search for parallels between the protest actions of 1968 and those of today and the recent past. There are some similarities, but just as significant, and probably more so, are the differences, as she also makes clear. Such differences should not deter us from studying 1968's "protests in the streets" as a means of shedding light on present-day issues and events. If we are to understand the course of the past five-plus decades and, thereby, place our current world into a fuller, more meaningful context, we must study the 1960s, with particular emphasis on the global protests and mass movements that placed an indelible stamp on that era and all that followed. The consequences of the events of 1968 were variegated and complex. In some cases courses taken and the choices embraced thereafter were done in conscious reaction to these upheavals.

Every time I walk by this KFC© delivery stand in Beijing, which is located next to a Western-style, five-star hotel that caters to the whims and cultivated tastes of China's new plutocrats and high-rolling entrepreneurs from around the world, I am reminded of how much China has changed since the Cultural Revolution, which Zachary Scarlett analyzes in Chapter 1. Yet the question I ask is: Would Colonel Sanders have come to China were it not for the Cultural Revolution? Certainly the economic reforms of Deng Xiaoping were intended to alleviate the economic disarray, institutional disorganization, and social dislocation occasioned by a decade-long Cultural Revolution—one might say a ten-year 1968. Still, without the shock of the Cultural Revolution, which uprooted much that was traditional—in some cases traditions stretching back more than 2,500 years—would the Colonel have found such easy access to China's markets? We will never arrive at a definitive answer to that question. What is certain is that, with over 3,800 outlets today in more than 800 cities throughout the People's Republic of China, KFC© chicken is by far the most popular fast food in the PRC, although it does come with spicy Sichuan sauce, rice, egg soup, and soy milk. The Cultural Revolution did not uproot everything.

Beijing Street Scene, 2010. Photo courtesy of Alfred J. Andrea.

In the arena of iconic images and popular culture, there are other signs of a reaction to the excesses of the Cultural Revolution. The ubiquity of Colonel Sanders' picture rivals that of Chairman Mao, whose portraits and statuettes are fast becoming collectors' items, and the revolutionary songs and dances of the Cultural Revolution championed by Mao's wife, Jiang Qian, are today largely nostalgic "oldies" performed for and by pensioners in China's many pleasure parks.

Whereas Scarlett focuses on a mass movement within a single nation and its ties to and disconnection from the larger world, Félix Germain uses a wide-angle lens to study Black protest across the Atlantic World in Chapter 2. Both historians are practicing world history in its truest sense, albeit with different approaches and perspectives.

As Germain points out, righteous anger over the toxic effects of abuses from the past—namely plantation slavery and colonial imperialism—fueled Black protests in France, Africa, and the United States. The immediate causes for anger were Jim Crow laws in the southern United States and more disguised but no less real forms of racial discrimination in the northern United States; neo-colonial mistreatment of West Indian and African workers in France; and a form of residual French cultural and institutional

Revolutionary Song and Dance in Beihai Park, Beijing, 2008. Photo courtesy of Alfred J. Andrea.

colonialism in the newly independent West African nation of Senegal. Much of this outrage is best understood against the backdrop of movements generated by Black artists and intellectuals from the 1920s and 30s onward, such as the Harlem Renaissance and the francophone *Négritude* movement, that celebrated Black cultural identity and condemned anti-Black racism in all of its forms. Added to that were certain phenomena of the late 1950s and early 1960s, mainly decolonization, the creation of

French Overseas Departments, and Civil Rights legislation and court decisions in the United States that sparked rising expectations within a number
of Black communities on both sides of the Atlantic. Those aspirations,
however, were not fully realized. The result in 1968 was a series of explo-
sive protests across the Atlantic World born of frustration and outrage. In
the United States, James Brown's 1968 funk song "Say It Loud—I'm Black
and I'm Proud" became a protest anthem, and it resounded through sub-
Saharan Africa as well, becoming a monster hit in Tanzania. In 1969, the
National Alliance of Liberals Party in the West African nation of Ghana
adopted the slogan "Say it loud. I'm NAL and Proud."

Complementing Germain's treatment of these trans-Atlantic protests
by people of color, Elaine Carey's Introduction focuses on the student
protest movements of the 60s in the United States that were nothing
less than frontal assaults on a triad of perceived American iniquities:
imperialism, militarism, and racism, as most vividly exemplified by the
war in Vietnam and an imbedded bigotry that denied African-American
citizens equality and dignity. As she points out in an essay that sets the
stage for the four chapters that follow, these protests ran the gamut from
the nonviolence advocated by Dr. Martin Luther King, Jr., to the Chicago
riots of 1968 and the Days of Rage of 1969. So far as anti-establishment
protest, both peaceful and violent, was concerned, 1968 was both a pivotal and a symbolic year, but as Carey points out, its roots extended far
back in time and its myriad manifestations went well beyond 1968.

Indeed, the United States of America was born in protest, and protest
has been part of the warp and weft of American culture for well over two
hundred years. My own state, affectionately referred to by some as the
People's Republic of Vermont, has more than its share of citizens who, in
addition to raising organic vegetables and goats, throwing pots, and making craft beers and ice cream, willingly protest anything and everything
from nuclear power plants to Wall Street. Causes such as decent wages
for University of Vermont service workers, the ethical treatment of ani-
mals, full-body scanning by the TSA, and auto–emission pollution have
occasioned periodic nude protests—imagine scores of naked students
and their not-so-young supporters on bikes. But that is another story.

Chapter 3 by Mauricio Borrero deals with the Eastern bloc protests of
1968 that erupted in Poland and the former nations of Czechoslovakia
and Yugoslavia. In these three Warsaw Pact nations, anti-Soviet protests
were centered respectively in Warsaw, Prague (in the present-day Czech
Republic), and Belgrade (in present-day Serbia). The one protest that

most caught the imagination of the West at the time and thereafter was the Prague Spring. As with all of the other protests of 1968 covered in this book, Borrero discusses both the failed but important antecedents of the Eastern bloc protests, such as the Hungarian Revolution of 1956, and, more important, their aftermaths.

Borrero is too good a historian to argue that we can draw a straight line of causation from the protest movements of 1968 to the successful revolutions of 1989 against Soviet domination, and the dissolution of the Soviet Union itself in 1991. What he does postulate, however, is the eminently reasonable thesis that the events of '68 discredited Soviet-style Communism both within the Eastern bloc and internationally. No longer was it possible to maintain that the Soviet Union could serve as an agent for structural change. The collapse of the Soviet Union's hegemony over Eastern Europe and its own demise two years later were not made inevitable by the events of 1968, but surely '68 stands out as a singular year in the chain of events that led to the implosion of the Soviet system.

The 1968 Olympic Games held throughout Mexico from October 12 to 27 served only as a backdrop to the massive social and political protests that preceded the games and which Elaine Carey studies in Chapter 4, "Mexico's 1968 Olympic Dream." Far more important to her story is "The Night of Tlatelolco" of October 2, when hundreds of protestors, many of them students, were killed by riot police and soldiers. Beyond the still-uncounted dead, hundreds of every age and both sexes were clubbed, and an unaccounted-for number were jailed, some of whom never reappeared. Ironically, the site, known as the Plaza de las Tres Culturas (Plaza of Three Cultures), was where, on August 13, 1521, tens of thousands of Mexica and their allies died at the hands of Spanish conquistadors and their Indian allies in the last stand of the Aztec Empire. Likewise, the massacre of 1968 effectively ended the wave of street protests and violence that two sets of student activists had set in motion in late July. Yet what had begun as a protest revolving around university issues and student concerns quickly evolved into a movement that challenged the government and involved persons representing a wide range of social classes, economic levels, and ages. As such, although suppressed, the movement and the resultant massacre were never forgotten. As Carey points out, 1968 was a significant moment in the process of loosening the iron grip on the nation enjoyed by the then-ruling *Partido Revolucionario Institucional* (PRI; Party of the Institutional Revolution). Significantly, after more than seventy years of ruling Mexico, the PRI lost the presidency to

Vicente Fox in 2000. The investigation into the Tlatelolco massacre and associated crimes launched by President Fox and subsequent prosecutions failed to satisfy many of the veterans of '68, but it was a beginning.

The 1968 street protests in Mexico City and the resultant massacre were of little interest to the average citizen in the United States. But one event that took place on October 16 in that city polarized Americans north of the Rio Grande and symbolized the great chasm that divided U.S. society and inspired so much of the protests there that Carey and Germain write about.

Following the finals of the 200-meter sprint, Tommie Smith and John Carlos, who ran first and third respectively in the event, ascended the award platform to receive their medals. During the playing of the "Star-Spangled Banner," both men bowed their heads and raised black-gloved fists in a Black Power salute. Without consideration for the peaceful nature of their act or the social-political context that motivated them, International Olympic Committee officials forced their immediate departure from "the Games." Reaction in the United States was mixed, but it probably is no exaggeration to state that most African Americans understood what Smith and Carlos wanted to convey by that salute, even if many disagreed with the tactic. Contrariwise, most other North Americans probably failed to understand or sympathize with the two athletes. The public outcry of criticism was immediate, loud, and sharp, and the two athletes were publicly vilified in many media. Each received more than a hundred death threats. Over the following forty years, however, attitudes and voices changed. In 2005, a twenty-three-foot statue of Smith and Carlos was raised on the campus of their alma mater, San Jose State University, as a tribute to two men who are now rightfully recognized as heroes of '68 who stood proudly for human rights.

All of us connected with the Critical Themes in World History Series present this book in the hope and with the expectation that all of its readers become more acutely aware of how much the world has changed since 1968 and how the global events of the "year" that stretched so far on both ends influenced that evolution. Indeed, this should be required reading for both those of us who lived through the days of '68 but insufficiently understood what was happening and why, and those for whom that year seems as ancient and foreign as the pivotal year of 1929 was to the students of 1968.

Alfred J. Andrea
Series Editor

ACKNOWLEDGMENTS

Years ago, I thought I would write a dissertation on how American, French, and Mexican student activists communicated, interacted, and perceived each others' activism. This idea emerged from my initial research on Mexican students in 1968, in which activists made numerous references to the American and French movements in their marches and interviews with the press. In the end, I decided to focus on the Mexican student movement, because little had been written about women (and little in English) on that movement. Since I published *Plaza of Sacrifices* in 2005, the scholarly body of literature on global 1968 has grown, and that growth has enhanced our knowledge of all aspects of these movements, whether they be their artistic, political, social, cultural, or economic impacts. *Protests in the Streets: 1968 Across the Globe* attempts to capture this growing body of literature for classroom use.

This book would not have been possible without the support of Alfred Andrea and Rick Todhunter. Al has nurtured this project for years, and Rick has offered a place for it to land and thrive. Charles Cavaliere, now at Oxford University Press, also played a key role in proposing the idea many years ago after he attended the conference "1968 in the World" at St. John's University in 2008. I also recognize the anonymous reviewers whose insights into the global 1960s improved the manuscript and challenged all of us, the writers, to expand our approaches. The University of New Mexico Press has graciously allowed me to reproduce materials from *Plaza of Sacrifices*.

I also wish to thank my colleagues in the History Department at St. John's University. As mentioned, this book emerged from a conference that the department hosted in 2008. Over the years, my colleagues have continued to discuss this project and offer their insights. Susan Schmidt Horning contributed to my musical knowledge of the era as well as the contemporary period. I also want to thank Nerina Rustomji, Sanae Elmoudden, and my student Sarah Eltabid, who gave me key insights into the events in the Arab Spring.

Over the years, my ongoing friendships with activists from the 1968 Mexican student movement continue to inspire me. Although I interviewed many activists in the period from 1995 to 1998, I continue to learn about the movement from friends and colleagues: Raúl Álvarez Garín,

Sandra Peña, Marcelino Perelló, Lucía Rayas Velasco, Ignacia "Nacha" Rodríquez Márquez, and José Agustín Román Gaspar. This work has also benefited from my long friendship with my mentor Enrique Semo Calev. He attended the conference in 2008 and gave the keynote address. In 1968, the Mexican government forced him into exile due to his political activism, and he spent much of that year in many of the countries mentioned in this book. His friendship, insights, and occasional criticisms have been invaluable in my evolution as a historian and scholar.

Elaine Carey

INTRODUCTION

Student Protests in the United States and Beyond in 1968

Elaine Carey

At the University of Virginia on April 12, 1968, Grayson Kirk, president of Columbia University, gave a speech in which he employed the phrase "the gap between the generations" to highlight the confrontation between youth and their elders that was a cultural facet of the 1960s. A few short weeks later, students, faculty, and administrators became immersed in a strike at Columbia University that splashed across the national media. Despite the ubiquitous nature of the phrase the "generation gap," Kirk's utterance understated the rifts between those in positions of authority and young people, many of whom expressed solidarity with people on the margins of society. Kirk's assessment that young people lacked respect for authority underscored a misreading of a rapidly changing world. Mark Rudd, a student leader at Columbia, rejected Kirk's analysis: "You call it the generation gap. I see it as a real conflict between those who run things now . . . and those who feel oppressed by, and disgusted with, the society you rule."[1] In many ways, Rudd's words seemed to echo around the globe, as the year 1968 became fraught with battles between young people and those in positions of power. More importantly, the suggestion that this global discontent arose out of a conflict between age groups—the "generation gap"—was misleading; the social reform movements that arose that year in various areas of the world were far more diverse, pervasive, and enduring in nature than they would have been had they amounted to nothing more than a group of discontented college students expressing disrespect for their elders.

The sociologist Immanuel Wallerstein characterized the pivotal year of 1968 as "one of the great formative events in our world systems, the kind we call watershed events."[2] Student activists constituted new political

---

1. Mark Rudd, *Underground: My Life with SDS and the Weathermen* (New York: Harper 2010), 54–55.
2. Immanuel Wallerstein, "1968: The Great Rehearsal," in *Revolution in the World System*, edited by Terry Boswell (New York: Greenwood Press, 1989), 19–20.

bodies that threatened power structures, whether one-party authoritarian regimes, bureaucratic communist polities, or democratic states. Yet the French philosopher Alain Touraine, a participant in the Paris strikes of 1968, argued that social movements cannot be separated from the culture in which they happened. Indeed, the movements under consideration here drew their inspiration from global shifts that took place in the 1950s and 1960s.[3] In accord with Touraine's theory, however, it is equally clear that all the movements embraced unique cultural icons and challenged indigenous political, social, educational, economic, and cultural structures. All the movements took dramatically different historical turns, and each continues to have a unique impact on present-day societies in different ways. In the years following 1968, many of the ex-activists entered into the political arena with shifting or maturing allegiances that at times led to criticism by their 1960s colleagues who remained supportive of the demands and issues of the past. In order to place the events of 1968 into their proper contexts and to understand fully the impact that they had on the course of history, we must study both global and local events as well as the motivations of the people who joined and led the protests and that of the authorities whom the activists challenged.

In considering the emergence of students as new political actors who joined with Leftists, Marxists, Maoists, Communists, and Nationalists in that pivotal year, the central analytical questions for this volume are: Why did young people across the globe mobilize against power structures, whether political, military, social, cultural or economic, at relatively the same historical moment? In what ways did these movements connect to such broader social movements, such as workers' rights, feminism, Civil Rights, the counter culture, the array of leftist concerns, and anti-colonial and anti-authoritarian impulses? Through which means did protesters demonstrate their resistance to internal conflicts and issues, and how did they defy national and cultural myths? Moreover, in the wake of 1968, what was the impact of the activists on politics, society, and culture? In other words, how did the protests of 1968 become a central part of the dramas inherent in the transformations that enveloped many countries? More importantly, why did the protests and movements of 1968 become

---

3. Alain Touraine, "De la mañana de los regimens nacional populares a la vispera de los movimiento populares," *LASA Forum* 28 (1997): 6–9. Also see his *The May Movement: Revolt and Reform: May 1968—the Student Rebellion and the Workers' Strikes—The Birth of a Social Movement* (New York: Random House, 1971).

an impetus for liberation, whether political, social, cultural, or sexual? Countering this image, Mao Zedong's Cultural Revolution anticipated and embraced these uprisings in part to consolidate power. In the wake of 1968, the world also witnessed a greater use of violent methods to bring forth change. For example, some former students took up armed struggle after certain governments employed violence against their attempts at peaceful and nonviolent change.

The United States in the World of 1968

Let us consider first the connections between the 1968 uprisings in the United States with those that swept other areas of the globe. The positioning of the United States as part of these global uprisings was incredibly important, because after World War II the United States emerged as one of two world superpowers. Compared to other industrialized countries, its economy expanded greatly in the early 1950s, although by the early 1960s other industrialized and developing nations experienced their own economic booms, including the defeated, largely destroyed, and then rebuilt and modernized nations of Germany and Japan. By 1968, as the United States enjoyed unprecedented prosperity, a general economic upsurge was affecting even developing countries, and Mexico appeared on the brink of entering the First World.

Postwar economic booms provided young people from across the industrialized world with an opportunity to attend universities. By 1967, over six million people in the United States attended universities and colleges (of that number more than two million were women), compared to a total of 1.5 million university and collegiate students in 1940. Not surprisingly, other industrialized nations also experienced greater access to higher education by the 1960s. Despite the earlier economic chaos in Europe in the immediate postwar era, by the 1960s young people flocked to universities in unprecedented numbers In France, for example, over half a million young people enrolled in postsecondary institutions. In Mexico, close to 150,000 students studied in colleges and universities, and women comprised 25 percent of the student body.[4]

---

4. United *Nations Statistical Yearbook: 1968* (New York: Statistical Office of the United Nations, Department of Economic and Social Affairs, 1969), 761. Organization of American States, *América en cifras: Situación cultural* (Washington, DC: OAS, 1968).

Moreover, the United States experienced profound national and global shifts in 1968; however, these changes had roots in the previous decades. The United States is frequently analyzed as having a separate or unique experience in 1968, when compared to the rest of the world. That supposed uniqueness was due, in part, to the fact that the United States' student movement took place in a large country with multiple locations of activism, such as Berkeley, Chicago, and New York. The large cities and universities were joined by regional activism such as in Ann Arbor, Seattle, and Tallahassee. The expanse of the student movement, with multiple centers of activism, led to a dispersed leadership and an array of protests.

In the United States and in much of the world, social activists in 1968 demonstrated a fatigue from the Cold War in which the United States played a central role. In some countries, especially Germany, young people questioned their parents' actions during World War II, while other 1968 activists challenged either the Soviet Union and its bloc nations or anti-Communist authoritarian governments. Others questioned U.S.-style capitalism. Students distrusted those in positions of power regardless of their ideology. A slogan emerged during the Berkley Free Speech movement that captured this perspective: "Never trust anyone over 30!"

Two events in the United States rippled across the globe. First, many activists in the United States' Civil Rights movement accepted U.S.-style democracy and capitalism, as they too wanted to ensure that all had equal access to the same American dream. Second, the United States' foreign policy, particularly in regard to the Cuban Revolution and the U.S. war in Vietnam, which began to escalate in 1964, served as a touchstone for many of the student protests across the globe. The murders of prominent leaders, such as John F. Kennedy on November 22, 1963, followed by Malcolm X on February 21, 1965, Martin Luther King, Jr., on April 4, 1968, and Robert F. Kennedy on June 6, 1968, rocked the United States, fueling rage against an establishment that seemed brutal toward its own citizens and foreign nationals alike, while incapable of protecting its leaders.

The Civil Rights movement, the Cuban Revolution, and the Vietnam conflict marked and radicalized the generation of 1968 in the United States. The New Left in the United States that emerged during the 1960s shared numerous characteristics with the New Global Left. In Mexico, France, and Eastern Europe, young people grew disenchanted with the rigid structures of the traditional left, which were based on Marxist-Leninist approaches that were established by the Communist International, which was an international organization that advocated for a social revolution, and that evolved from the Russian Revolution. Younger leftists demanded greater participatory democracy, bringing them into conflict with many older leftists. Whereas, in China, Mao Zedong found offensive Nikita Khrushchev's 1956 denunciation of Josef Stalin's cult of personality, in Mexico and France, to the contrary, Khrushchev's comments offered the left, particularly young members who were not tarnished by Stalinism, other models of socialism and communism. Likewise, internal struggles within the Left emerged in the United States. Jeremy Suri has argued that such large institutions as governments, bureaucracies, and their media arms also contributed to a sense of insignificance among the young.[5] For many young people, that feeling of insignificance also included their place within the party structures of what was being referred to as the Old Left.

The 1950s and early 1960s offered young people a sense that they could bring change by working with local activists hoping to construct a new society. African-American students in the Deep South organized sit-ins at lunch counters to protest segregation. On February 1, 1960, four students at North Carolina A&T State University, Joseph McNeil, Ezell Blair, Jr., Franklin McCain, and David Richmond, led the first lunch counter sit-in at the Woolworth store in Greensboro, North Carolina, which became a model for other young activists.[6] As sit-ins spread across the Deep South, the confrontations grew more violent. As early as 1961, activists from the North joined voter registration drives in the Deep South. These activists included Mario Salvo, Tom Hayden, Marshall Ganz, Mary King, and Casey Hayden, who continued their activism into the late 1960s; several of them later emerged as leaders and spokespeople for the student movement.[7] In February 1968, National Guardsmen killed three students and wounded fifty others at South Carolina State College after students protested a Whites-only bowling alley. Just a few short weeks later, Martin Luther King, Jr., arrived in Memphis to support

5. Jeremy Suri, *The Global Revolutions of 1968* (New York: W.W. Norton, 2007), xvi.
6. See *February One: The Story of the Greensboro Four*, produced by Steven A. Channing, Rebecca Cerese, Cynthia Hill, and Daniel Blake Smith (Video Dialog, 2004), 61 mins.
7. Salvo was one of the leaders of the Berkeley Free Speech movement. Tom Hayden was one of the founders of SDS and wrote the *Port Huron Statement*. Ganz was a member of the Student Nonviolent Coordinating Committee (SNCC), a civil rights organization composed of students, workers, and activists and worked with the United Farm Workers. Mary King and Casey Hayden were members of SNCC and issued one of the earliest feminist statements in the emerging student movement.

sanitation workers who were trying to organize a union. King's dream of nonviolence to combat segregation ended when he was murdered. In the wake of King's assassination, people rioted and over forty cities across went up in flames, leading the governors to activate the National Guard to restore order and protect citizens and property. Violence flared on both sides, with gun battles breaking out between National Guard soldiers and armed civilians. While certain leaders blamed the riots solely on King's murder, the riots of the late 1960s developed due to the simmering rage that many dispossessed urban people felt toward the police, the government, the lack of opportunities in the inner city, school inadequacies, and housing discrimination, as well as King's murder. Though the riots gave people an opportunity to vent their frustration and rage at a system, they inadvertently harmed many other citizens.

Recent scholarship on the U.S. Civil Rights movement traces the origins of the movement to the early-to-mid-1900s, and considers such early protesters as the Pullman Porters (who organized a union in 1925) and the women who led the Montgomery bus boycott in 1955 as its true founders. Their struggles became a model for organizing nonviolent protests, and activists around the globe embraced their methods. However, by 1968, many activists in the United States wondered if nonviolence was working. Beginning in 1966, we see the rise of more militant methods embraced by groups who had initially organized around nonviolent principles, such as the Student Nonviolent Coordinating Committee (SNCC) and the Black Panthers. This shift to violence also had a global impact.

Young people in the United States and around the world drew inspiration from King and other activists. International journalists captured the marches and demonstrations in text and video, and ordinary people from around the globe created their own forms of media in new newspapers, broadsides, and other publications. These periodicals and newspapers took a more radical anti-war stance than that which existed in the mainstream media. Young people in the so-called Eastern bloc, which consisted of the Soviet Union and its satellite nations, as well as in France, Mexico, and elsewhere, watched news clips of, and read newspaper accounts about, such events as Commissioner of Public Safety "Bull" Connor's attacks on civil rights demonstrators in Birmingham, Alabama, or the Tet Offensive (launched on January 30, 1968), but they also shared information about their own movements and transnational ties and alliances through media such as student newspapers, posters, and magazines.

By 1968, the student-led U.S. Civil Rights movement had changed. In the late 1950s and early 1960s, young people had sought societal change by participating in voter-registration drives such as the Freedom Summer of 1964, which sought to register African-American citizens in Mississippi and other states in the Deep South. Such direct experiences connected to the emerging student movement of the later 1960s, because young people had criticized the political and power structures not only within the South but also across the United States. They also had tremendous influence with the federal government. Presidents Eisenhower, Kennedy, and Johnson sought to integrate schools and colleges and protect voting rights. Students who participated in Freedom Summer also gathered at a state park in Lakeport, Michigan in 1962, adopted the *Port Huron Statement,*[8] elected officers, and reinvigorated the Students for a Democratic Society (SDS). Founded in 1959, SDS grew out of the Intercollegiate Socialist Society (ISS) and the League of Industrial Democracy associated with the United Autoworkers (UAW). Hence, the meeting at Port Huron took place at a UAW camp. With the formation of SDS, the *Port Huron Statement* explicitly expressed solidarity with a number of struggles, some of which would gain momentum in the 1970s: the Civil Rights movement, anti-nuclear proliferation, and anti-colonialism.

Though the *Port Huron Statement* began as a public experimental questioning of the United States, it captured the sentiments of a certain group of disaffected global youth that questioned all power structures. In its early years, SDS focused on civil rights and community organizing through the Economic Research and Action Project (ERAP). ERAP, which evolved into the activist arm of SDS, organized the urban poor in thirteen projects in low-income neighborhoods in Chicago, Boston, and Newark. This "coalition of the poor" aimed to eradicate poverty by organizing the unemployed, most of whom were men. Despite an initial focus on these unemployed men, ERAP activists eventually began to work more closely with women. Even though ERAP disbanded in the late 1960s, the organization left a legacy. At the first meeting of the National Coordinating Committee of Welfare Rights Groups, held in Chicago in 1966, twenty-six delegates came from ERAP programs. Activists employed diverse tactics for community organizing that continue to be used into the present such as community organizing from the micro-level that

---

8. https://www.lsa.umich.edu/phs/resources/porthuronstatementfulltext (accessed March 22, 2016).

addressed the needs of the community.[9] In some SDS chapters, however, members focused on strictly university-related issues, such as restrictive residency requirements, restrictive hours for women, and dress codes.

As the war in Vietnam escalated in the later 1960s, and as the Civil Rights movement became increasingly militant, many activists shifted their focus to the Vietnam War, condemning it and equating segregation to the treatment of the Vietcong—a stance that enraged the establishment. Further, anti-war activists, who connected the war in Vietnam to inequality and racism within the United States, saw their own struggles as one with those for civil rights and liberties around the world, whether they be in the United States, France, Ireland, or the Soviet Union. With the escalation of the war in Vietnam, SDS affiliates across the United States also concentrated less and less on internal issues at universities and embraced the anti-war movement. By 1965, SDS organized "teach-ins" across the country that served to mobilize young people to the anti-war movement, using methods that its leaders had learned from Civil Rights activists in the Deep South.

In 1965, SDS called upon students to march on Washington to protest the Vietnam War. One of the leaflets they circulated stated:

> Our aim in Vietnam is the same as our aim in the United States: that oligarchic rule and privileged power be replaced by popular democracy where the people make the decisions which affect their lives and share in the abundance and opportunity that modern technology makes possible. This is the only solution for Vietnam in which Americans can find honor and take pride. Perhaps the war has already so embittered and devastated the Vietnamese that that ideal will require years of rebuilding. But the war cannot achieve it, nor can American military presence, nor our support of repressive unrepresentative governments.[10]

Many SDS members grew skeptical of organizational control. This fear of centralized leadership resulted in a splintering of the group into diverse organizations and the dispersal of SDS leadership across the United States. The escalation of the war, along with heightened

9. Jennifer Frost, *An Interracial Movement of the Poor: Community Organizing and the New Left in the 1960s* (New York: NYU Press, 2005), 176.
10. Students for a Democratic Society, "Bring the War Home," in *The Sixties Papers*, edited by Judith Clavir Albert and Stewart Albert (New York: Praeger Press, 1984), 247–53.

xxii   *Introduction*

government surveillance of the antiwar movement, further contributed
to the breaking up of SDS. Consequently, by 1966, formal membership
in SDS had declined. Jane Alpert, a radical involved in bombings of NYC
buildings, recalled in her autobiography that she approached a SDS
recruiter and activist telling him she wished to join. He replied, "Nobody
joins SDS. That will get your name on an FBI list. . . . If you want to get
involved, why you don't you go to this meeting." He handed her a flyer for
the Community Action Committee at Columbia University.[11]

SDS moved toward this type of decentralized organization particularly after its leaders met with Vietcong leaders in Cuba in January of
1968. The decentralization grew in part out of fear of infiltration by the
FBI, which had proven itself capable of surveillance of civilians during
the Civil Rights movement. SDS modeled much of its leadership on
what was taking place elsewhere in the world. Across the globe, activists
expressed their admiration for guerillas, whether in Vietnam or Cuba,
and applied their organizational methods. In France and Mexico, countries with a revolutionary past, organizational methods demonstrated
a questioning of authority and a suspicion of centralized leadership. In
turn, activists in both Mexico and France adopted for their organizations
a cell-like structure that allowed them to address the needs of different
protests and social movements.

Irving Howe, a leftist intellectual, has argued that a fear of leadership
led to disorganized and chaotic meetings. Howe, one of the founders of
the Democratic Socialists of America and *Dissent* magazine, recalled a
SDS meeting he attended in New York: "Two ideas were being tested
here: that decisions be reached not by vote but by consensus, and the role
of the leaders be kept to a strict minimum." He concluded that the meetings were tedious, attaining few goals.[12] Further, in his essay, "New Styles
in Leftism" published in 1965, Howe castigated the New Left's ideas
about participatory democracy as shallow and anti-intellectual. He also
expressed concern about their enthusiasm for Mao Zedong, Fidel Castro,
and Ernesto Che Guevara, as well as other Third World revolutionaries.[13]

In many ways, Howe's criticism foreshadowed the demise of the New
Left in the United States. But for young radicals, Howe was simply

---

11. Jane Alpert, *Growing Up Underground* (New York: William Morrow, 1981), 15.
12. Irving Howe, *A Margin of Hope* (New York: Harcourt, Brace, Jovanich, 1982), 293.
13. Irving Howe, *New Styles in Leftism* (New York: League for Industrial Democracy,
1965).

another voice of the establishment, criticizing the youth movement. The New Left, represented by the student activists and their supporters, saw the Old Left, such as Howe, as ineffectual and inactive. In the United States, this phenomenon of deep distrust of the previous generation differed from the experience of activists in other parts of the world, where rebellious young people often found support from many different quarters. Opposition party members, union leaders, workers, artists, parents, teachers, professors, professionals, and others joined with young men and women to protest their governments, demonstrating that the mantra commonly uttered in the United States, "Never trust anyone over 30," did not extend across the globe as a common attitude of protest. Indeed, in Mexico student activists relied on their parents, many of whom joined them in their demonstrations against the government. In China, however, Mao Zedong saw the youth as the vanguard of his own continuing revolution, and he encouraged young people to engage in open criticism of their elders who undermined him and the Cultural Revolution.

The Columbia Strike

Although many important events took place in the United States during 1968, two events stood out as highlights of the clash between young people and those in positions of power: the strike at Columbia University and the protests at the Democratic National Convention in Chicago. The strike led to certain successes, but the protests in Chicago merely served to demonstrate the emerging fractionalization within the New Left. With the war in Vietnam intensifying in 1968 in the face of North Vietnam's Tet Offensive, student strikes became a tool to bring about changes on university campuses. Universities received federal funding for research that then was employed by the military. Protests against the Reserved Officer Training Corps (ROTC) and military-directed research gave students on-campus targets that they connected to Vietnam. (Of course, it must be noted that military-based research routinely adds significant benefits to the civilian world, such as jets, computers, and even cell phones.)

The first student strike of 1968 took place at Howard University when students took over the administration building. They demanded that the president resign, that a Black Studies program be formed, and that certain students not be expelled. Howard activists used the language of the Civil Rights movement to demand curricular changes in a politically heated moment. They received support from countless other student activists across the United States, including those at Columbia University, and the strike at Howard ignited strikes at other campuses.

In April of 1968, students at Columbia University went on strike, occupying five buildings, including the president's office in the Low Library. The students used the protest, which took place almost three weeks after the assassination of Martin Luther King, Jr., to voice a number of SDS demands, including an end to university funding of military research and the ROTC, and the consideration of the rights of Harlem residents as the university sought to expand the Columbia campus into that neighborhood. (The university planned to build a gymnasium for its students in Harlem.) The Columbia protesters connected the university's ties to the defense industry with its plans to build new structures in Harlem. As one student expressed it:

> We have taken power away from an irresponsible and illegitimate administration. We have taken power away from a board of self-perpetrating businessmen who call themselves trustees of this university. We are demanding an end of the construction of the gymnasium, the gymnasium being built against the will of the people of the community of Harlem, a decision that was made unilaterally by powers of the university without consultation of peoples whose lives it affects. We are no longer asking but demanding an end to all affiliation and ties with the Institute for Defense Analysis,[14] a Defense Department venture that collaborates the university into studies of kill and overkill that has resulted in the slaughter and maiming of thousands of Vietnamese and Americans.[15]

Despite warnings from university administrators, students occupied buildings, took a vote, and elected to strike. They barricaded themselves

---

14. The Institute for Defense Analysis was a consortium of twelve universities that carried out research for the Department of Defense.
15. The Newsreel, *Columbia Revolt*, 1969, 59 mins. DVD. 2008. Also see the transcript "Forty Years After Historic Columbia Strike, Four Leaders of 1968 Uprising Reflect," *Democracy Now*, http://www.democracynow.org/2008/4/25/forty_years_after_historic_columbia_strike (accessed October 1, 2010).

inside the administration buildings and organized defense committees. The university as a physical site provided students with an array of supplies to further the strike. Students communicated by walkie-talkies, used office equipment to mimeograph their statements, and took various administrators as hostages. SDS students went to the various dorms to hold group discussions on the strike; Black students took Hamilton Hall and renamed it Nat Turner Hall of Malcolm X University. Feminist activist and scholar Kate Millet has written: "The strike transformed Columbia, made it wonderful for a time: ideas came alive, faculty debates were high drama, and principles were at issue. The academy reasserted itself, drew away from government and business, existed for a while on its own terms."[16] While Millet captured the sentiments of some students, others felt that the strike undermined their ability to engage ideas: classes were cancelled, and the campus was occupied by activists and police.

Students from the other colleges and universities in the area joined their Columbia peers. Because of its location in New York City, the strike drew immediate local and global attention. The *New York Times* covered the strike, but also decried it as being "organized by extremist forces within SDS that sabotaged any constructive course to discuss their grievances."[17] *New York Times* reporter Steven V. Roberts, a liberal-leaning journalist, mentioned that Mark Rudd, the leader of SDS, frequently quoted revolutionary slogans that he "picked up on a recent trip to Cuba."[18]

On April 27, 1968, the NYPD massed officers onto the Columbia University grounds to occupy every building that had not already been taken by the students. To ensure that the strikers' numbers could not grow, the police worked closely with university administrators in sealing off the campus to everyone but students, faculty, and the media. The police established checkpoints at key entrances onto the campus, but university president Grayson Kirk requested that they exercise restraint when dealing with the students. On April 28, the board of trustees commended the restraint of the administrators and police. As in many parts of the world, those in positions of power used certain media outlets to craft their messages. The board argued that it halted construction of the

16. Kate Millet, *Sexual Politics* (Champaign, IL: University of Illinois Press, 2000), xvi.
17. "Hoodlumism at Columbia," *New York Times*, April 25, 1968.
18. "Sit-in Spectrum Has a Wide Range," *New York Times*, April 25, 1968.

gym, thereby addressing a key demand of the students. Yet the board's members continued to express their belief that a minority of students had disrupted the academic freedom of the majority.[19]

Despite a police presence and the halting of construction in Harlem, people continued to join the strike. H. Rap Brown and Stokely Carmichael of SNCC easily passed through the checkpoints to join the protest. They were interviewed live on WKCR, the student radio station. Correspondents sent by WKCR to the different occupied buildings reported on major developments through live pick-ups.[20] Campus radio stations offered the students a voice to the world when other forms of media outlets were broadcasting only the statements of politicians and university administrators. University or "guerrilla" radio became a tool of communications for young people across the globe.

In the early morning of April 30, the police maneuvered to remove students from the buildings. The police used the tunnel system, common to many universities, to enter certain buildings and retake them. The students offered resistance, but the police subdued them. Although the strike came to an end, it had already attained some key elements of success: it halted the construction of the gym, secured Kirk's resignation, and established solidarity, though fragile, between Black and White students. In November, students from the Third World Liberation Front challenged the administration in a four-month struggle that led to the formation of Ethnic Studies at the university. Like the Howard strike, the Columbia strike became a bellwether for other university protests. Students across the United States went on strike to demonstrate their discontentment with the decision-making processes in many universities. Student strikes broke out across the United States as far as California, with activists demanding similar programs and protesting military-based research. After 1968, those strikes and actions became more violent. In 1970, the bombing of Sterling Hall at the University of Wisconsin in Madison by four young men opposed to the Vietnam War led to the death of Robert Fassnacht, a thirty-three-year-old physics researcher and father of three young children, who was working in the building that night.

---

19. "Text of Columbia Trustee's Position on the Protest," *New York Times*, April 28 1968.
20. "Radio: Keeping Abreast of the Turmoil at Columbia," *New York Times*, April 27, 1968.

The Democratic National Convention

Throughout 1968, the New Left had planned to bring people to Chicago to protest the nomination of Lyndon B. Johnson. However, the events of the spring of that year forced a change in tactics. Many young people felt demoralized over the political situation in the wake of the assassination of Robert "Bobby" Kennedy, who was President John F. Kennedy's brother and attorney general. Many asked, what is the point in trying to change the world? Johnson's announcement in March that he would not seek re-election in 1968 had been another remarkable event in a year marked by the assassinations of key leaders, a heightened war, and the growing influence of a counterculture.

All of the energy generated by these events came to a head in Chicago, which had a recent history of violence against antiwar demonstrators in April of 1968. Moreover, Chicago had tense racial relations throughout the 1960s. The Yippies (Youth International Party), the National Mobilization Committee to End the War in Vietnam (a coalition of anti-war organizations known as "Mobe"), and the Black Panther Party joined SDS in Chicago. The Yippies formed in 1968 and used a theatrical style to demonstrate dissent. College faculty and activists formed Mobe in 1966 to try to focus more attention on the Vietnam War. These organizations advocated more direct action such as draft-card burning. Other groups advocated more aggressive forms of resistance. SDS made a similar move to the left when it elected Bernardine Dohrn, a declared revolutionary communist, as its figurative leader. Dohrn expressed her solidarity with the North Vietnamese, and that statement did not sit well with police and city officials in Chicago who knew of the coming protest. In Chicago, Dohrn and other members of the Revolutionary Youth Movement (RYM), took control of SDS. The RYM, which also included Mark Rudd from Columbia University, changed its name to the Weathermen, a term coined by Bob Dylan and part of the title of a RYM manifesto.[21]

---

21. Bob Dylan, "Subterranean Homesick Blues," on *Bringing It All Back Home*, Columbia Records, 1965. "You Don't Need a Weatherman to know which Way the Wind Blows," submitted by Karin Asbley, Bill Ayers, Bernardine Dohrn, John Jacobs, Jeff Jones, Gerry Long, Home Machtinger, Jim Mellen, Terry Robbins, Mark Rudd, and Steve Tappis, *New Left Notes* (June 18, 1969), https://archive.org/stream/YouDontNeedAWeathermanToKnowWhichWayTheWindBlows_925/weather_djvu.txt (accessed March 17, 2016).

As people gathered in Chicago, the Yippies sought publicity through such outrageous stunts as running a pig ("Pigasus the Immortal") for president and threatening to put LSD into the Chicago water supply. At the same time that the Democratic National Convention and protests were taking place, Soviet tanks rolled across the Czech border, adding to a growing atmosphere of tension. Despite their efforts to challenge the pro-war stance of the Johnson administration and the Democratic Party, the activists failed. The Democratic Party announced its support for the war in Vietnam; both parties, therefore, had a war platform. The antiwar candidate Eugene McCarthy—who had the activists' support—lost the nomination to Hubert H. Humphrey, Johnson's hand-picked candidate.

Outside of the convention hall, the tension between police and activists reached a crescendo. As the police and activists clashed, the press captured images of police marching into the crowds armed with clubs and rifles. Television viewers saw police beat children, the elderly, and bystanders. Police dragged women by their hair and turned on the press, not realizing that other cameras were capturing their assaults. The organizers urged the demonstrators not to fight back or struggle as the crowd chanted, "The whole world is watching! The whole world is watching!" But fighting broke out between the students and the police, with both sides attacking one another. Contrary to the desire of the main organizers of the protest, many groups who went to Chicago had long planned to fight in the street. Activists taunted the police with expletives and threw whatever materials they could find.

The Rupturing of Connections

The violence further added to the polarization among Americans. Some supported police actions against "hippies," while others decried the violence against the protesters. With the violence, student protests continued and escalated across the nation, but so too did the surveillance of activists. Black Panthers, SDS, and Mobe activists increasingly found themselves to be targeted by the Federal Bureau of Intelligence's Counter Intelligence Program (COINTELPRO). COINTELPRO, created by the FBI in 1956 during the Red Scare, lasted until 1976, when the U.S. Senate's Church Committee (the United States Senate Select Committee to Study Governmental Operations with Respect to Intelligence Activities) exposed its illegal and unconstitutional practices. In the 1960s, and until its demise, the program investigated political activists in the Civil Rights movement, the New Left, and the Black Panther Party, in particular. Sociologists Jack Whalen and Richard Flaks have written:

> The FBI and other intelligence agencies carried out programs of harassment and surveillance of questionable legality. Such activities were widely publicized, and ultimately a paralyzing paranoia spread through the youth and student communities. Youth questioned whether the risk of extreme physical danger was a reasonable price to pay for confrontation with authority.[22]

The impact of COINTELPRO inspires debate among many 1960s activists to this day.

Universities and activist organizations became sites of infiltration. The FBI documented benign behavior as well as more extreme acts. Students and professors were photographed at demonstrations protesting, for example, speeches given by General William Westmoreland, the former commander of all U.S. forces in Vietnam (1964–1968). The FBI also documented the collaboration between U.S. students and other revolutionaries. In October 1967, the National Liberation Front, the political arm of the Vietcong, announced the formation of the Vietnamese Committee for Solidarity with American People. New committees were created in other parts of the world to promote solidarity between movements in the developing world. U.S. activists traveled to Czechoslovakia to meet other anti-war activists from around the world and demonstrate their solidarity with the Vietnamese. They also traveled to Vietnam and to Cuba. For most activists, these trips served to garner a greater understanding of the revolutionaries, but in some cases, they underwent training. Though actress Jane Fonda, who visited North Vietnam in 1972, would become the most famous (or infamous) U.S. visitor to that country during the war, other anti-war activists had already traveled to meet North Vietnamese officials in other countries. These meetings contributed, in part, to an ideological shift from nonviolence to more aggressive tactics.

---

22. Jack Whalen and Richard Flask, *Beyond the Barricades: The Sixties Generation Grows Up* (Philadelphia, 1989), 115. See also Ward Churchill and Jim Vanderwall, *COINTELPRO Papers: Documents from the FBI's Secret War Against Domestic Dissent* (Boston: South End Press, 1990, rpr. 2011).

Following the violent confrontations at the Democratic National Convention, SDS continued to escalate its acts of violence into 1969. The rise of the Weather Underground, which evolved out of the Weathermen, and a turn to violence contributed to the fractionalization and ultimate collapse of SDS. Having been trained abroad in insurgency methods, the Weather Underground and other organizations hoped "to bring the war home." On October 8, 1969, young people armed with pipes, wearing helmets and other forms of body protection marched through parts of Chicago destroying private property. The Weathermen argued that they must bring the war home so that Americans would understand what was taking place in Vietnam. The march culminated with a riot in Lincoln Park. The three-day-long Days of Rage, as it became known, occurred as the Chicago Seven, those seen as leaders of the riots in 1968, went to trial.[23] The Days of Rage, the rise of the Weather Underground, and increasing violence led young members of the movement to criticize the shift away from nonviolent methods to effect social change.

Many of the activists' actions in 1968 and 1969 did not have the desired effect of galvanizing the American populace to see things their way. We must remember that Republican Richard Nixon won the presidency in 1968 and won again—overwhelmingly, with over 60 percent of the popular vote—in 1972. Nixon's two elections clearly demonstrate that a large portion of the American population did not share the students' vision. Many Americans were appalled by the violence that became a tool of the New Left in the wake of 1968, the shifting cultural mores regarding sexuality and drug use, and the societal changes that were taking place.

The heightened violence led many to question the movement and its fixation on using violence to end the war in Vietnam. Other activists, especially women, gained greater traction in 1968 and the following years. Women long active in civil rights work and the student protest movement became increasingly critical of their roles within both movements. In 1968, a significant number of such women of the Left articulated the claim that sexism existed within both movements, as well as within U.S. society at large. They not only questioned the division of labor but also demanded equal access to education, work, and opportunities. Their experiences with the changing sexuality of the times led

---

23. The Chicago Seven included Rennie Davis, David Dellinger, John Froines, Tom Hayden, Abbie Hoffman, Jerry Rubin, and Lee Weiner. Bobby Seale, a Black Panther, was given a separate trial date. The Chicago Seven is also known as the Chicago Eight.

them to assert that women must control their own bodies and have access to information regarding birth control regardless of age and marital status. In turn, greater access to the birth control pill began in 1968, not only in the United States but also in other parts of the world. Feminists also questioned the private division of labor within the household, by demanding that men participate in the raising of children, and they advocated for communal childcare and communal kitchens.

Nonviolent organizing methods to achieve the goal of ending the Vietnam War continued and new groups emerged. The Vietnam Veterans Against the War (VVAW), formed by six veterans in New York City in June 1967, brought a different background to the anti-war movement. Their opposition to the war grew from their personal experiences in Vietnam. Though many of these vets came from socioeconomic backgrounds that were dramatically different from those of the students of 1968, the VVAW as a whole had clear ties to the student movement: among its earliest members were Columbia University graduates who had served in the war. In the early years, members of the VVAW presented a distinctly more conservative appearance, wearing short hair and donning suits. Over the next five years, however, the VVAW became more radicalized by the counterculture as well as by its struggle to expose the U.S. military's secret bombings of Cambodia, and the VVAW's clean-cut image shifted to one more closely resembling that of the student protesters. They wore their hair long, all or part of their combat battle dress uniforms, and their medals and decorations. In 1971, John Kerry, a highly decorated naval hero of the war and a future senator, presidential candidate, and secretary of state, appeared before the Senate Foreign Relations Committee (which, coincidentally, he would chair many years later) representing the VVAW and testifying about what was taking place in Vietnam and why the war needed to end. Such veterans in the movement played a significant role in mobilizing mass opposition to the war. Vietnam veterans protesting the war often found themselves criticized, and at times ostracized, by their fellow Korean and World War II veterans; yet at other times, some of these older veterans joined their protests to address the differences between the wars.

The student movement's use of the rhetoric of freedom, democracy, and the focus on criticizing power structures has found a place in many of today's contemporary social movements in the United States. The women's, LGBTQ (Gay, Lesbian, Bisexual, Transgender, and Queer), Latino, and American Indian movements, as well as the development of ethnic studies departments and gender and women studies departments, all trace their origins to the protest movements of the 1960s.

Global Student Protest Movements

China, France, the Caribbean, West and East Africa, Eastern Europe, and Latin America also experienced profound social upheavals in 1968. All activists participated in a global moment of history, and yet each place had distinct demands unique to the country and its history. In other words, the global met the local in 1968. The following chapters examine the contingencies and contradictions of the 1968 students' movements, considering them as global protests that yielded dramatically different local consequences. In China, Mao Zedong saw students as the perfect group to coalesce with at an opportune time in order to gain greater control within the party and over the country by furthering revolutionary principles while removing critics from the intelligentsia and bourgeoisie. In France and Senegal, West Indian and Senegalese activists looked to the American Civil Rights movement as a model when they took to the streets to challenge the French Empire as a shameful and outdated concept that further marginalized Black people within France as well as in its colonies. In Eastern Europe, localized demands for freedom from the power of the Soviet Union offered an opportunity that was brutally repressed only to re-emerge in the 1980s. In Mexico, the Olympic Games—a truly global event—served to highlight internal dissent that had been brewing for years. These movements were part of a global moment but with profound differences and more localized demands—all of which were far more complex than a simple generational conflict.

Chapter 1

The Cultural Revolution: China's "Global" Rebellion[1]

Zachary Scarlett

On May 25, 1966, Nie Yuanzi and a group of students from the Philosophy Department at Beijing University hung up a poster accusing the school's administration of suppressing the masses and abnegating Mao Zedong's revolutionary line. So began China's Great Proletarian Cultural Revolution (1966–1976), a movement that plunged the country into a ten-year period of chaos that tore families and communities apart and brought the country to the brink of civil war. By the end of this period, two million people had been killed and an immeasurable number of people suffered psychological and physical injury. For the first two years of this campaign China's young people took center stage, acting as the vanguard of the Cultural Revolution. Between 1966 and 1968, university and senior middle school students (grades 10–12) became one of the most powerful collective forces in China, partially dictating the direction of the Cultural Revolution. In the process, these students temporarily disassembled the basic power structure that had dictated daily life in the People's Republic of China, fought each other for control of the movement, destroyed countless numbers of China's most precious artifacts and historical sites, and managed to alienate almost every sector of Chinese society.

One cannot, however, solely focus on the students when studying the Cultural Revolution. In every student action lay the designs of Mao Zedong and his close allies, including his fourth wife, Jiang Qing, and

---

1. While each of the other chapters in this volume specifically discusses an event or series of events that occurred in 1968, this chapter covers a broader time period. Although events in France, Mexico, and Czechoslovakia came to a head in 1968, other parts of the world did not follow the same pattern. West Germany, for example, saw more civil unrest in 1967 than it did in 1968. Similarly, the Cultural Revolution had reached its denouement in 1968, instead of its peak. For the purposes of this chapter we may therefore consider "1968" in a broader perspective—as a representation of the radicalism that embodied political movements around the world in the latter half of the 1960s, and not just in a single year.

1

the head of the People's Liberation Army, Lin Biao. It was this powerful clique in the Chinese government that gave the Chinese students the resources and, indeed, the impetus to rebel. The origins of the Cultural Revolution lay in domestic and international developments and in Mao's growing sense of dismay with Chinese society. Before the start of the Cultural Revolution, Mao began to suspect that members of the Chinese Communist Party (CCP), even those in positions of power, were conspiring to restore capitalism in Chinese society. Mao was also concerned that the next generation of China's leaders—those who came of age in the 1960s—were unprepared to take the reins of the Communist state. The Cultural Revolution was supposed to be a cure for both ailments. Mao had two primary goals during the Cultural Revolution. First, he wanted to eliminate his enemies in the CCP. Second, Mao also wanted to forge the Chinese students' revolutionary ideology in the fires of an intense political campaign. The Cultural Revolution, therefore, empowered Chinese students; at no time since the Communist revolution in 1949 did students wield so much influence in Chinese society. And yet, for all of their ostensible autonomy, it was Mao Zedong's words that guided the students' actions and adorned their revolutionary posters. While the students may have challenged the CCP's authority, they never came close to dislodging Mao's grip on Chinese society.

It may, therefore, seem strange to include the Cultural Revolution in a study of the student movements that swept the world in the 1960s and early 1970s. The Cultural Revolution was unlike any other movement that arose during this period—in magnitude, course, and shape. During the 1960s, there was no equivalent to Mao Zedong, nor did any other protest movement reach the level of violence that was visited on Chinese society during the Cultural Revolution. Even where revolutionary organizations did commit acts of violence, in places such as Italy, Germany, and the United States, they did not compare to the destructive ferocity of the Chinese students and others who joined with them.

And yet the Cultural Revolution was not an island, nor was it completely isolated from the rest of the world in the 1960s. What instead emerged was a type of dialogue between Chinese students and their global counterparts, one that was fueled by actual contact as much as it was by an active imagination. Foreign revolutionaries and activists visited China during the Cultural Revolution, and many more turned to China as a revolutionary alternative to the Soviet Union. For their part, Chinese students—who called themselves the Red Guards[2]—kept abreast of revolutionary activities elsewhere, read the French Marxist philosopher Sartre, and followed the Civil Rights movement in the United States. Many student newspapers also contained exaggerated stories about how Mao Zedong's theories about revolution were changing the world, and how the students themselves were setting an important example for all others to follow. Chinese students and the CCP often co-opted and distorted the 1960s, making it appear as if the Cultural Revolution and Mao Zedong were central figures in the impending global revolution again the capitalist and imperialist system. When examining the place of the Cultural Revolution in the 1960s we must therefore walk a fine line between reality and imagination. The Cultural Revolution was connected with the rest of the world, and influenced (and was influenced by) foreign student movements. This fact, however, should never obscure the differences between the Chinese experience and other foreign student movements, or the fact that Chinese students often mixed reality and imagination to create a 1960s that only occasionally mirrored the actual decade.

Origins

The People's Republic of China (PRC) was founded on October 1, 1949. Over the next seventeen years, China experienced its fair share of radical campaigns, turbulent politics, and crises of various kinds. Although the origins of the Cultural Revolution can be found in the basic fabric of the PRC, it was the disaster of the Great Leap Forward and the Sino-Soviet split that sowed the seeds of the movement. The Great Leap Forward was a campaign launched by Mao Zedong to modernize China and rapidly turn the PRC into a world power. However, his policies, which required unscientific agricultural methods and the breakneck industrialization of the countryside, led to disaster. Between 1958 and 1961, the Chinese economy was in a state of total disrepair. The famine that ensued from the policies of the Great Leap Forward cost

---

2. Most Red Guards were students, but they were not the sole participants in the Cultural Revolution. There were factory organizations, *danwei* (work-unit) activists, and picket brigades, to name several nonstudent groups that were active during the Cultural Revolution. In Shanghai, for example, factory workers, not students, were the primary vehicles of the Cultural Revolution.

roughly thirty million lives.[3] Mao and his policies were largely discredited, and he temporarily relinquished the power to make day-to-day decisions while his compatriots attempted to right the economy. Two high-ranking officials, Liu Shaoqi and Deng Xiaoping, took over the daily responsibilities of running the state. Their new policies were less radical than Mao's economic theories, and both Liu and Deng tended to favor small family farms over the big and unwieldy communes of the Great Leap Forward. Although the economy did recover, Mao eventually became concerned that both Liu and Deng's new policies would lead to a restoration of capitalism in China.

The second critical event, the Sino-Soviet split, was a slow-boiling diplomatic crisis that first developed in the 1950s and then reached a point of open rupture in 1961 when Beijing denounced the Soviet leaders as "revisionist traitors." As the world's two largest Communist states, China and the Soviet Union were natural allies. Joseph Stalin, the premier of the Soviet Union, was an important source of support in the early years of the PRC. However, with Stalin's death in 1953, relations between the two powers began to disintegrate. Stalin's replacement, Nikita Khrushchev, was highly critical of his predecessor's tactics, which Mao found offensive. Mao had partially based his own rule on Stalin's reign in the Soviet Union, and he believed that any criticism of Stalin was a personal attack. The two leaders also had very different worldviews, which were influenced by the Cold War détente of the later 1950s. In an attempt to decelerate the bellicose rhetoric of the early Cold War, Khrushchev declared that capitalist and communist states could peacefully coexist. This idea was antithetical to Mao's core theories: Mao believed that the communist states could not rest until all capitalist states were eliminated. For Mao, détente was capitulation.

Mao preached "permanent revolution" and fretted over the ideological stagnation that would accompany any prolonged period of peace. In the late 1950s and early 1960s, Mao came to believe that the leadership of the Soviet Union had abandoned Communism for a revisionist policy. This policy abnegated world revolution and instead advocated gradual modernization under Moscow's guidance. Such a policy, in his view, left the imperialist powers free to continue their abusive policies in Asia, Africa, and South America. Even worse, Mao came to believe that the Soviet Union

---

3. For an in-depth study of the Great Leap Forward see Frank Dikotter, *Mao's Great Famine: The History of China's Most Devastating Catastrophe, 1958–1962* (New York: Walker and Company, 2010).

was no better than its capitalist enemies, and that Moscow was another imperialist wolf in communist clothing. The détente of the Cold War never reached China, and Mao kept the country on permanent high alert. Now that the Soviet Union, once China's most powerful ally, had abandoned the cause of permanent revolution, Mao was forced to look elsewhere for allies. For Mao, the Sino-Soviet split taught him of the dangers of abandoning revolution and embracing the comfort of stability and ossification. The only way to avoid such a fate was by launching wave after wave of tough political campaigns that ensured the ideological purity of the Chinese people and strengthened the country's anti-imperialist credentials.

In response to the failures of the Great Leap Forward and the disasters of the Sino-Soviet split, Mao began to search out new partners, both foreign and domestic. Internationally, Mao continued to stress Third World solidarity and the anti-imperialism of the People's Republic of China. Mao stressed that China was the only large revolutionary state left that favored the immediate liberation of the Third World. Domestically, Mao relied on Lin Biao and Jiang Qing to consolidate his power. Subsequently, Lin Biao required that each Chinese soldier study *The Quotations of Chairman Mao*,[4] while Jiang Qing demanded a more militant Maoist approach to Chinese culture, especially in literature and the performing arts. As Lin and Jiang accrued more power, Mao began to articulate the problems he believed Chinese society faced. Chief among his critiques was that the party had abandoned many of his most radical policies. After witnessing what had happened in the Soviet Union, Mao was concerned that officials in China were undermining the Communist revolution with a revisionist approach to politics and the economy. He believed that Chinese society had become too complacent and had abandoned class struggle in favor of comfort. A new political campaign was needed to rectify this situation.

Mao, however, was too smart to attempt a frontal assault, and instead decided to attack his enemies by criticizing China's artists and intellectuals. In January, 1965, Mao urged officials to undertake a "cultural revolution," declaring that certain artists were reactionaries, revisionists, and capitalists who used culture to express anti-Maoist sentiments. He

---

4. *The Quotations of Chairman Mao*, known as the "little red book," became one of the ubiquitous symbols of the Cultural Revolution. Red Guards waved the book at rallies to demonstrate that Mao's theories were guiding their actions. The book was also popular in Europe and the United States, where the Black Panthers sold the book in the Oakland–San Francisco area to raise money for their organization.

was joined by Jiang Qing, who had long believed that cultural circles had become bastions for Mao's enemies, and that certain members of the CCP had actually patronized and protected these reactionaries. Despite his call for a "cultural" revolution, it is clear that Mao's true targets were those officials in the party whom he believed harbored capitalist sentiments. In order to purge the cultural field and expose the reactionaries in the CCP, Mao ordered the publication of a series of editorials criticizing certain artists. The first of these editorials appeared on November 5, 1965, in a Shanghai newspaper, and claimed that Wu Han, the vice mayor of Beijing and a prominent playwright, had used the arts to criticize Mao Zedong and the Communist Party. Although hardly anyone knew it at the time, the Cultural Revolution had begun.

Strangely, nothing happened. None of the country's major newspapers reprinted the article. Most officials in the Communist Party responded cautiously. Many likely knew, however, that the winds of a new political campaign were stirring; coming out strongly for or against the article could put one at great risk in the future. Eventually, five officials were put in charge of investigating the claims against Wu Han. The head of this group was Peng Zhen, the mayor of Beijing and a high-ranking member of the CCP. Soon after the article's publication, Peng decided to treat the matter as an academic case to be debated by scholars and cultural critics. Peng likely had no idea that Mao Zedong was behind the publication of the article. His moderation ended up being his downfall. In the spring of 1966, Mao called an enlarged meeting of the Political Bureau of the Communist Party of China's Central Committee (popularly known as the Politburo) and criticized Peng Zhen and his allies for their slow response to the editorial and for muting the new political campaign. Peng was removed from power and replaced by Jiang Qing. Jiang in turn surrounded herself with some of the most radical members of the party, forming a powerful new clique in the CCP that was committed to expanding the scope of the Cultural Revolution. Peng's removal from power meant that the Cultural Revolution would extend well beyond the arts, just as Mao had planned from the beginning.

The Students

Mao was an old revolutionary, and he knew that launching such a massive campaign against powerful officials in the Communist Party required the support of the masses. In order to assure this support, Mao turned to

"Smash the old world, build a new world." <chineseposters.net> number BG D29/184 (IISH collection).

an unlikely source: Chinese students. Students had played a major role in Chinese politics in the twentieth century. However, the heyday of the students came before the Communist Revolution in 1949. Afterward, students' role in society diminished, and youth were expected to look to the peasantry and the proletariat for inspiration. The Cultural Revolution, however, was different. When the winds of a new political campaign began to blow, the students responded, first in Beijing and then around the country. In the spring of 1966, students became swept up in the moment, captivated by a romantic notion of revolution and an almost religious love for Mao Zedong. Why did the students respond so enthusiastically? Some were genuinely dissatisfied with the direction of Chinese society, particularly new education policies that had been recently implemented. For many of China's youth, however, there was a deep sense of longing for a significant revolutionary experience. Many students looked upon their parents and elders in the CCP as the liberators of China. What would this new generation accomplish? Some students began to feel that the revolutionary moment of their parents had passed them by. The Cultural Revolution was a golden opportunity for China's youth. According to Mao, the country was once again under siege from capitalists, counterrevolutionaries, and imperialists, just as it was in the first half of the twentieth century. If a new generation could help eliminate this dangerous element in Chinese society, then the students could make the same mark in history as their parents had. It was the opportunity that many had waited for.

As previously noted, the students of Beijing University were the first to respond to Mao's call for revolution. On May 25, 1966, students in the Philosophy Department, led by Nie Yuanzi, a party representative at the university, hung a "big character poster"[5] denouncing the school's president Lu Ping for obstructing the Cultural Revolution. The poster would quickly become a popular form of criticism during the Cultural

---

5. "Big character posters" were one of the most ubiquitous and effective means of denouncing a so-called capitalist or enemy of Mao Zedong during the Cultural Revolution. These posters varied in length, but often followed a familiar pattern. The author (or authors) would first declare their support for Mao and the Cultural Revolution, and they would accuse any number of people of abnegating Mao Zedong Thought or conspiring to restore capitalism in China. Later, rival Red Guard groups would use these big character posters to accuse their enemies of adulterating the Cultural Revolution. Every inch of free space on college campuses and factory walls was often filled with these big character posters during the Cultural Revolution.

Revolution, and this first one claimed that Lu and others had conspired to undermine the masses and take control of the Cultural Revolution. Chaos ensued at Beijing University; soon hundreds of posters appeared, both defending and criticizing Lu Ping. Even more important, students were beginning to discuss the meaning of the Cultural Revolution, which had finally moved out of the upper echelons of the party and into the streets.

The leadership of the Communist Party responded to the flurry of big character posters with great confusion. Mao Zedong was not in Beijing at the time the first poster was hung and so did not give immediate instructions on how to respond. There was also a split within the party between those who encouraged radicalism and those who did not completely approve of the students' actions. Several officials had known about the first big character poster at Beijing University before it was hung, and even though students worked on the text of the poster, officials close to Mao approved the final version. Still, these radical officials had to use caution and ensure that the student movement did not get out of hand. Several days after the first poster appeared at Beijing University, the top leadership of the Central Committee decided to send work teams to all of Beijing's major senior middle schools and college campuses. These work teams were composed of trusted Communist cadres who were charged with directing the nascent student movement. While party members may have talked about mass mobilization, what many of them wanted was to control the students.

The Student Rebellion

On June 4, 1966, Liu Shaoqi and Deng Xiaoping, who were still in charge of the day-to-day operation of the state, flew to Hangzhou, a city in the south of China where Mao Zedong was vacationing, to update him on the situation in Beijing. They informed Mao about the big character posters at Beijing University and the party's decision to dispatch work teams to university and senior middle school campuses. Mao was noncommittal on the work teams, neither praising nor condemning the decision. But while the party leadership debated what to do next and how to decipher Mao's true feelings, the students pressed on in their struggle to carry out the revolution. On May 29, 1966, a dozen students from the senior middle school attached to Tsinghua University in Beijing held a clandestine meeting and formed the first official Red Guard unit of the Cultural Revolution.[6] Others followed suit, and soon student Red Guard units roamed the streets of Beijing. The problem, however, was that there was no consensus on how to conduct the Cultural Revolution. Instead, students formed into different Red Guard factions, each with its own interpretation of the Cultural Revolution. One of the most important initial disagreements among the different Red Guard groups was what to do about the work teams. Should the students demand that they themselves control the Cultural Revolution, or should they accept guidance from the work teams? This question would consume the students in the opening months of the Cultural Revolution.

Those who composed "radical" Red Guard units had resisted the authority of the work teams from the start. This resistance had turned into outright rebellion on some of Beijing's major campuses, including Tsinghua University. Led by the outspoken student Kuai Dafu, students at Tsinghua University began to denounce the repression of the work teams. In turn, the work teams began to resort to authoritarian tactics. Many of the work teams coerced radical students to spy on their classmates. Kuai himself was placed under house arrest. Elsewhere, the conflict between the work teams and the Beijing University students became so intense that the campus was shut down, and the most outspoken students were instructed to scrape provocative big character posters off of the walls. The conflict gathered steam throughout the summer, and neither the radical students nor the government seemed willing or able to reach an agreement. As Kuai wrote on June 21 in a big character poster, "we must all ask ourselves, revolutionary leftists, whether the power now in the hands of the work team represents us. If it does, then we should support it; but if it doesn't, then we should seize power once again."[7]

It took Mao Zedong himself to finally break the logjam. After remaining silent for most of the summer, Mao returned to Beijing in August and moved quickly to consolidate his power and to use the radical students to his advantage. On August 5, 1966, Mao published his own big character poster entitled "Bombard the Headquarters" (see the sources at the

---

6. Most major universities in China have an attached middle school, which encompasses what would be equivalent to the 8th to 12th grades. In this case, it was middle school and not university students who formed the first Red Guard unit. Chinese historians translate this school as "Tsinghua Attached Middle School."

7. Quoted in Roderick MacFarquhar and Michael Schoenhals, *Mao's Last Revolution* (Cambridge, MA: Harvard University Press, 2006), 72.

end of this chapter), which praised the rebellious students and criticized those in power who had suppressed their movement. Although he did not mention Liu Shaoqi or Deng Xiaoping directly, it was clear that they were Mao's main target. The response to Mao's big character poster was immediate. The work teams were withdrawn from all campuses, and the radical Red Guard groups were vindicated. The victory of the students encouraged others around the country to join the Cultural Revolution. The movement soon expanded beyond the capital and became a national event. Mao's support of the radical students also meant trouble for Liu Shaoqi and Deng Xiaoping, who soon lost their positions in the Communist Party. Liu was placed under house arrest, while Deng was sent to labor in a factory. Both men were reviled by the students, and articles appeared daily in many student newspapers denouncing Liu and Deng. What had begun as a small intellectual debate had now, with the help of the students, morphed into a major political campaign.

Free from the control of the work teams, the Red Guards unleashed a torrent of chaos in which hardly anyone was safe. In August and early September 1966, a reported 1,722 people were killed, either at the hands of the Red Guards, or, under threat of attack by the Red Guards, by suicide. Much of this violence was the result of intense struggle sessions in which supposed enemies of the people were ordered to confess their crimes. Victims were often accused of being anti-Party, harboring secret capitalist sentiments, or conspiring against Mao Zedong. Some Red Guards even turned on their own families and accused them of traitorous acts. Many Red Guards also took the opportunity to settle old scores, accusing those who had personally wronged them in the past of political crimes. The accused who resisted or those who did not appear sincere in their confessions were often physically harmed. Students also tried to humiliate their victims. Some were criticized for previous sexual relationships. Women in particular became a target for their supposed promiscuity. Victims were also made to wear large dunce caps or placards around their necks, which listed their crimes. Students ransacked homes and destroyed countless historical sites and artifacts. Many students viewed ancient Chinese culture and history as a backward vestige of the past. To many, traditional culture was tantamount to backward superstition, and needed to be eliminated if China ever hoped to develop into a truly egalitarian society. Eventually students began to expand the Cultural Revolution beyond Beijing, after being afforded free passage to travel on the nation's rail system so that they could spread the

Cultural Revolution across the country. At first, the targets of these Red Guards were school officials, teachers, and lower party representatives, whom many students believed had conspired to stifle the movement. For students, those in authority had been shockingly derelict in their political duty, and had allowed China to slip into a revolutionary lethargy. The students' aim was to eliminate anyone who was not wholly committed to Mao Zedong or his revolutionary principles. Many students needed to look no further than school administrators, whom they believed had designed curriculums that did not focus enough on politics, and had built an educational system that excluded poor peasants. Although they began with lower officials and school teachers, students soon began to criticize powerful bureaucrats and senior party officials. The Red Guards quickly became indispensable in executing Mao Zedong's revolutionary vision.

The January Power Seizure and the Wuhan Incident

During the winter and into the summer of 1967, Chinese students and their patrons inside the CCP expanded the Cultural Revolution. After eliminating university officials who had supposedly advanced an anti-party educational system, Mao and the students set their sights on the bureaucracy, an institution that Mao reviled. In Shanghai, during what became known as the January Power Seizure, workers and students overthrew the municipal government and formed what was ostensibly a new revolutionary committee led by the masses. Although the central government continued to monitor and influence events in Shanghai, the student-worker alliance had essentially taken control of the city. Students in Beijing followed suit, and some even demanded the formation of a new revolutionary alliance whose members would be elected by the masses. During this period, students also began to discuss the Paris Commune of 1871—a failed attempt by radical Parisians to overthrow the French government—as a historical model that they could emulate, and the term appeared regularly in both student and national newspapers.

In reality, however, China's communes never quite resembled the short-lived Paris commune, which was renowned for its democratic principles. Mao quickly ordered two of his closest allies to take control of the situation in Shanghai. Furthermore, the experience in Shanghai could not be properly replicated anywhere else in China. The attempt to

"Seize Power," as an editorial in the official newspaper of the CCP, the *People's Daily*, intoned, was only accomplished in five other provinces. Most Red Guards were mired in factional infighting. No consensus emerged on how to seize power from the bureaucrats and the local government, and the party soon moved to restore stability. When the experience of the January Power Seizure proved more complicated than Mao had foreseen, he slowly backed away, choosing to maintain some small modicum of order instead of allowing for the possible destruction of local authority.

One of the factors that made power seizures even possible in the first place was support from the local army. Without the army's support, new revolutionary committees found it difficult to overcome factionalism and establish a new government. And yet the army had a difficult time fitting into the Cultural Revolution. On the one hand, soldiers were ordered to aid the students in their efforts to drag out capitalists and overthrow the old power structure. On the other hand, the army was a bureaucratic and rigid organization; revolution was the antithesis of its basic structure, despite Lin Biao's efforts to inculcate Maoism within its ranks. In 1967, in an attempt to rectify the army's tenuous position in Chinese society, the CCP urged the students and other cadres to join forces with the People's Liberation Army (PLA) and continue the Cultural Revolution. The students, however, came to increasingly resent the influence of the army, and cracks in this new alliance emerged almost immediately.

Tension between the army and China's radical students was laid bare in the city of Wuhan, one of China's most important industrial centers. For much of 1967, Wuhan was a city divided. Factional struggles began in January 1967, when the Wuhan Workers' General Headquarters, composed of radical students and unskilled laborers, attempted to seize power from the Wuhan city government. The Million Heroes, an alliance of skilled workers, conservative students, and state employees, opposed the Wuhan Workers' General Headquarters.[8] The Million Heroes were able to defeat their opponents mainly because they were supplied with weapons by the local army general, Chen Zhidao. Despite the success of the Million Heroes in January, violence did not abate in Wuhan. By

---

8. Here, the term "conservative students" refers to those students who participated in the Cultural Revolution but chose to defend various power structures in the Communist Party. In Shanghai, for example, conservative students resisted the overthrow of the city government. Many conservative students also tended to support the work teams that were dispatched to college campuses when the Cultural Revolution began.

the summer of 1967, the situation in the city became so perilous that the central government in Beijing intervened, ordering General Chen to withdraw his support for the Million Heroes. But Chen demurred and the situation became more dangerous. Eventually Beijing dispatched two high-level officials to Wuhan in an attempt to persuade Chen to obey orders and to negotiate a truce between the two factions. Once again, however, Chen and the Million Heroes proved defiant. On the night of July 20, the Million Heroes kidnapped one of the negotiators. Army officers soon surrounded the villa of the second negotiator, effectively placing him under house arrest. What began as a factional fight had quickly escalated into a serious situation. Conservative students had colluded with the army in an attempt to evade a negotiation that would have empowered the radical faction in the city. Resentment between the radical students and the army grew, as both sides felt that the other was trying to take control of the Cultural Revolution in Wuhan. After some heavy-handed threats from Beijing, General Chen and the conservative students finally released the two negotiators, who returned to Beijing as heroes. The members of the Workers' General Headquarters were heralded as true revolutionaries, while the Million Heroes and the leadership of the Wuhan military were disgraced. In the midst of all this chaos and factionalism thousands of students were arrested, wounded, or killed during the violent clashes that engulfed Wuhan.

Radicalism and the End of the Red Guards

Outraged by the army and the conservative students' actions, officials in Beijing reacted with a call to "arm the left." Jiang Qing urged rebel students to "attack with reason, defend with force."[9] Later that summer, on July 31, 1967, *Red Flag*, the leading radical newspaper during the Cultural Revolution, published an editorial entitled "The Proletariat Must Firmly Grasp the Barrel of the Gun."[10] This new radicalism manifested itself most dramatically in foreign affairs. Many of China's foreign embassies were shut down, and Chinese foreign diplomats were recalled to China in order to take part in the Cultural Revolution. In China, Red Guards held

---

9. MacFarquhar and Schoenhals *Mao's Last Revolution*, 214–15.
10. Maurice Meisner *Mao's China and After: A History of the People's Republic*, 3rd edition. (New York: The Free Press, 1999), 338.

protests in front of several foreign missions. Meanwhile, Chinese living abroad attempted to spread the Cultural Revolution abroad. Students in the Soviet Union clashed with Soviet police after they attempted to hold a rally in Moscow. In Indonesia, Chinese were expatriated or killed as the government became increasingly nervous about their revolutionary influence on Indonesian society. In China, some radical officials, including those allied with Jiang Qing, began to criticize the Foreign Ministry for being insufficiently radical. These officials believed that the Foreign Ministry was full of useless bureaucrats who appeased capitalist and revisionist foreign governments.

Concurrent with the new influence of radical officials in foreign policy was a new focus on the issue of Hong Kong. Hong Kong had been ceded to the British in 1842 after China's defeat in the First Opium War (1839–1842). The city had become a constant reminder of China's humiliation at the hands of the Western powers during the nineteenth and twentieth centuries. In the midst of the Cultural Revolution, British colonialism in Hong Kong became a particularly galling issue. In July 1967 a group of Red Guards began to assemble in front of the British Mission in Beijing to protest the British occupation of Hong Kong.[11] These protests lasted through July and August. Events finally came to a head on August 22, 1967, when Red Guards stormed the mission and burnt part of the building to the ground. For the students, their actions were an example of the vigilance and commitment to revolution that was so prized during the Cultural Revolution. For many officials, however, it was a sign that China was on the verge of anarchy.

One such official who was outraged by the students' actions was Zhou Enlai, China's second-in-command and a respected diplomat and official. Zhou criticized the students' actions, and was backed up by Mao Zedong. Mao took two dramatic steps in order to stave off anarchy: he purged several high-ranking officials, and he ordered the PLA to restore order in China. In October 1967, Mao went even further and called for a great alliance, demanding that the students halt their factional battles, turn in their weapons, and accept an alliance with Communist cadres and

---

11. "Missions" are diplomatic representatives of the governments of foreign countries. They are usually considered to be one step below embassies. When one government wants to maintain contacts with another government, but not necessarily approve of that government's reign, it will often establish a mission rather than an embassy. In this case, the government of Great Britain maintained a mission in Beijing in order to maintain lines of communication without condoning the Communist government in China.

the army. The radicalism that had resulted from the Wuhan Incident and the attack on the British embassy proved too dangerous for Mao and his colleagues. Once again they turned to the army for help.

Not all students, however, were prepared to cede power to the army. In an effort to cajole the students into submission, Mao ordered the formation of Mao Zedong Thought Propaganda Teams—composed mostly of factory workers—to move onto school campuses and restore order. Still students resisted. At Tsinghua University, Kuai Dafu ordered his classmates to defend their campus. Five members of the Propaganda Team were killed by Tsinghua students, and many more were injured. Furious, Mao summoned the leaders of Beijing's Red Guards to the Great Hall of the People for a meeting. At the meeting, Mao informed the students that their actions were unacceptable. To ensure their acquiescence, Mao soon decided that members of the largest and most troublesome Red Guard units would be banished to the countryside to rectify their thinking and learn from the peasantry. The urban Red Guard movement was essentially over, and China's students were dispersed and exiled to the country's remotest province. For the next eight years, many would remain there, toiling under difficult conditions.

Despite the fact that the Cultural Revolution did not officially end until Mao's death in 1976, the movement took on a different shape after the Red Guard movement was broken. Although violence did not abate (in fact, more people died after the students were sent down to the countryside than before), the rest of the Cultural Revolution was consumed with factionalism in the CCP, mutual recriminations, arcane and esoteric political debates, and a slow attempt to return China to a state of normalcy.[12] During this time, Mao had to strike a balance between stability and revolution. Completely abandoning the Cultural Revolution would have meant admitting that the movement, the violence, and the carnage had all been for naught. Instead, he kept the Cultural Revolution alive, while rejecting most of the radicalism that characterized the first years of the movement.

---

12. Some of the worst violence came in 1969 during the Cleanse the Class Ranks campaign. All over China people were abused and murdered during this campaign, which was meant to eliminate any troublemakers from the new revolutionary committees that had replaced the students. For a description of the violence of this campaign, see MacFarquhar and Schoenhals, *Mao's Last Revolution*, 256–60.

Still, problems abounded for Mao and the leadership of the CCP. There was perhaps no bigger crisis than Lin Biao's attempt to overthrow the government in 1971. This event shocked people both inside and outside of the government. After all, Lin's place in Chinese politics seemed assured; his name was even written into the new Chinese constitution as Mao's chosen successor. Why would he attempt to overthrow the government? It seems that by 1971 Lin began to doubt that he would actually succeed Mao. Lin was troubled by the many enemies that he had accrued in the CCP, and suspected that perhaps Mao, despite his public declarations, would choose one of his rivals to be his successor. During the summer of 1971, Lin Biao and his son began to plan the overthrow of the government, and even discussed Mao's assassination. But for reasons not known, the planned coup d'état never materialized. Lin quickly gathered his family and fled China. His plane, however, crashed over Mongolia, reportedly because his hasty departure meant that the pilots had taken off without a full tank of fuel. All aboard were killed, and thereafter Lin was vilified as a traitor.

Although Lin's death was not officially announced until much later, the events of 1971 proved too difficult for many people to accept, and support for the Cultural Revolution, even among some of its most zealous adherents, declined. The horror of this period and the realization of the movement's futility caused some in China to reconsider Maoism. And yet, that did not erase the Cultural Revolution's psychological scars that remained (and still remain) for many. Today the Cultural Revolution is a taboo subject in Chinese society, and the government has offered little recognition or compensation for those who were affected by the movement. Moreover, the Cultural Revolution largely discredited many of Mao's most radical theories. By the end of the movement in 1976, it became clear that even the Chinese people were exhausted by Mao's policies. When Zhou Enlai died early in 1976, an outpouring of grief marked his passing. Although a consummate ally of Mao Zedong, Zhou was viewed as a moderate voice. He was seen as a counterweight to Jiang Qing and the radicalism of the Cultural Revolution, and when masses gathered to mourn Zhou's loss, it was a clear sign of their preference for stability over extremism. Later in 1976, Mao Zedong himself passed away. Soon after, Jiang Qing and three of her associates were arrested and accused of attempting to usurp power. Labeled the Gang of Four, each powerful official was found guilty of committing crimes during the Cultural Revolution and were essentially blamed for the entire fiasco. After the arrest of the Gang of Four, Deng Xiaoping, who was twice purged during the Cultural Revolution, miraculously assumed the leadership of the Communist Party and adopted a much more moderate and eventually capitalist position. Deng, having personally witnessed the extremes of Mao Zedong Thought, opened the country to foreign trade and embarked on a long series of reforms, which have made China one of the most powerful countries in the world today. Still, the effects of the Cultural Revolution have not abated. While the party and the country have long moved past the radicalism of Mao Zedong, many of the wounds opened during this period have yet to heal.

The Cultural Revolution in the World

The Cultural Revolution was unlike any other political or cultural movement that took place in the 1960s. However, that does not mean that China was completely isolated during the Cultural Revolution. Instead, both official publications and student newspapers incorporated the protest movements of the 1960s into their revolutionary discourse. The Chinese government also actively promoted the Cultural Revolution abroad. This was especially true in the Third World, which the Chinese Communist Party considered to be China's natural ally. China positioned itself as the champion of the Third World, offering an ideological model for leftist Third World revolutionaries. And yet China did not compromise its revolutionary ideals. While the CCP attempted to cultivate a better relationship with the Third World, the party also demanded that foreign governments and radical organizations abroad recognize the superiority of Mao Zedong Thought. Sino-Indian relations, for example, remained strained in the 1960s, not only because of border disputes between the two countries, but because of India's generally cordial relationship with the United States and the Soviet Union. In response, Beijing actively supported pro-Maoist groups in India. In order to inspire these revolutionaries, the CCP dropped copies of Lin Biao's *Long Live the People's Victory* from a plane over India. Written in 1965, this essay was one of the foundational documents in the Cultural Revolution, urging vigilance and the need for continuous revolution. This was all part of the CCP's new revolutionary strategy, which stressed an anti-Soviet and anti-American worldview, and emphasized the new importance of global revolution, anti-imperialism, and the Third World.

The global dimensions of the Cultural Revolution were unlike the internationalism expressed in many Western countries. While students all over the world engaged in an open debate about the meaning of youth, democracy, equality, and racial justice, Chinese internationalism took on a paternalistic tone. Chinese students and the CCP believed that the Cultural Revolution was a model for all other revolutionary movements. They framed the 1960s in such a way as to reaffirm the superiority of Mao Zedong Thought. Global events were often mediated to fit the reality of the Cultural Revolution. In particular, Chinese propaganda lauded Mao's global importance during the Cultural Revolution. One such propaganda poster urged the Chinese people to "resolutely support the anti-imperialist struggle of the Asian, African, and Latin American people."[13] Another poster read, "American imperialists, get out of South Vietnam."[14] Still another poster filled with well-armed revolutionaries (one individual appears to represent the Middle East, another represents the African continent) urged people around the world to unite "and defeat the American invaders and their running dogs."[15] These posters, however, mixed internationalism with Chinese Communist symbols. In the corner of each of these propaganda posters was the image of the red sun, a symbol that stood for Mao Zedong's reign in China. Mao embodied all of the characteristics of the red sun: not only its consistency, but also its power and its place in the sky. So powerful was this image that several student newspapers carried a section titled "Mao is the Reddest Sun in the Hearts of the World's Revolutionaries."[16] These propaganda posters suggested that the Cultural Revolution was a movement with international consequences, and that Mao was the unquestioned champion not only of the Red Guards but also of the myriad revolutionary movements of the 1960s.

---

13. Lincoln Cushing and Ann Tompkins, *Chinese Posters: Art from the Great Proletariat Cultural Revolution* (San Francisco: Chronicle Books, 2007), 100.

14. Ibid., 99.

15. Ibid., 103.

16. "Mao zhuxi she shijiegemingrenminxinzhong de hongtaiyang," *Waishihongqi* (May 26, 1967), in Song Yongyi, *Xinbian Hong wei bing xi liao* (Oakton, VA: Center for Chinese Research Materials, 2001), 11,855.

A translation of the Chinese is: "Resolutely support the American people in their resistance against American imperialist aggression in Vietnam." See chineseposters.net number BG E15/838 (Landsberger collection).

The internationalism of the Cultural Revolution was also expressed in the anti-imperialist rhetoric of both the Red Guards and the CCP. Officials and students often identified imperialists as one of the main targets of the Cultural Revolution, and sometimes accused supposed capitalists of also abetting global imperialism. Both student and official newspapers reported on what they perceived to be examples of the imperialist intent of foreign countries, especially the United States. The Atlas Publishing House in Shanghai published *The Atlas Fighting Papers*, which identified exactly where anti-imperialist struggles were taking place all over the Third World. In this context, the Vietnam War took center stage in China during the 1960s and was used to reinforce the importance of the Cultural Revolution. The war was framed as another imperial operation launched by the United States to serve its capitalist ambitions at home (a charge with which many Western activists heartily agreed). An article in the *Peking Review*, the official English language paper of China, declared that "The 700 million Chinese people who are armed with Mao Tse-tung Thought[17] most resolutely support their Vietnamese brothers in resisting U.S. aggression to the end."[18] At a rally held during the Cultural Revolution, students carried signs that read "China is behind Vietnam."[19] Gao Yuan, a former Red Guard who wrote one of the first memoirs about the Cultural Revolution, recalls participating in a play in which three students dressed as an American soldier, sailor, and pilot confessed their crimes in Vietnam.[20]

A key component of the internationalism of the Cultural Revolution came in the form of Mao's global image. During the Cultural Revolution, Mao was presented as both a national and an international leader. The *Peking Review*, for example, published pictures of armed Congolese citizens posing around a picture of Mao.[21] Red Guard newspapers often evoked the idea that Mao Zedong Thought was the "beacon" of the world's revolutionary people. Chinese diplomats serving abroad were

17. Mao Tse-tung is simply an older way of spelling the name Mao Zedong in Roman characters.
18. "Statement of the Chinese Foreign Ministry on the New Developments in the Vietnam Situation," *Peking Review* 10, No. 11 (March 10, 1967): 12.
19. Yang Kelin, *Wenhua dageming bowuguan* (Hong Kong: Dongfangchubanshi, 1995), 502.
20. Gao Yuan, *Born Red: A Chronicle of the Cultural Revolution* (Stanford, CA: Stanford University Press, 1987), 66.
21. *Peking Review* 11, No. 19 (May 10, 1968): 16.

instructed to distribute Maoist propaganda; several of these diplomats were expelled from Kenya for this act. The prospect of global revolution in the 1960s therefore provided both students and the CCP with a means to portray Mao Zedong Thought as the only ideology suited to meet the challenges of overcoming capitalism, imperialism, and the strictures of the Cold War. Viewed through the eyes of the Red Guards and other participants in the Cultural Revolution, it was Mao Zedong's revolutionary ideology and the shining example of the Cultural Revolution that inspired the global radicalism of the 1960s.

Despite the overblown way in which the Red Guards portrayed Mao's international influence during the Cultural Revolution, certain radical groups outside of China did incorporate Mao Zedong Thought into their movements. In West Germany and France, students and activists read Mao Zedong's work and debated the meaning and course of the Cultural Revolution. Some declared themselves to be devoted Maoists.[22] In Latin America, Maoism was popular throughout the continent, although activists often reconfigured Mao's ideas so that they would better fit with local situations.[23] And in the United States, some members of the Black Panther Party eagerly engaged with Mao and the Cultural Revolution. The CCP similarly offered support to the Black Panthers and received several of the group's members on their official visit to China in 1969 and again in 1971. Many in China believed that African Americans were the key to the overthrow of the U.S. government. In 1968, the Atlas Publishing House distributed a map entitled "The African-American struggle against violent oppression." The map detailed over one hundred American cities in which African-American protests and riots had taken place, and declared that within the "20 million black Americans there is an extremely strong revolutionary force."[24] On the back of the map were affixed adhesive strips, so that the owner could hang the poster on his or her wall and contemplate America's racial injustice.

---

22. For a description of Maoism in West Germany, see Quinn Slobodian, *Foreign Front: Third World Politics in West Germany* (Durham, NC: Duke University Press, 2012). For a description of Maoists in France, see Richard Wolin, *The Wind from the East: French Intellectuals, the Cultural Revolution, and the Legacy of the 1960s* (Princeton, NJ: Princeton University Press, 2010).

23. Matthew Rothwell, *Transpacific Revolutionaries: The Chinese Revolution in Latin America* (New York: Routledge Press, 2013).

24. Lincoln Cushing and Ann Tompkins, *Chinese Posters: Art from the Great Proletarian Cultural Revolution* (San Francisco: Chronicle Books, 2007), 99.

For their part, the Black Panthers constantly praised Mao Zedong and his revolutionary ideology. *The Black Panther*, the official newspaper of the Black Panther Party, published quotations from Chairman Mao alongside articles about community development and the progress of the Black struggle in America. The Black Panthers' relationship with China was partly shaped by personal experience. Robert F. Williams, the author of *Negroes with Guns*, lived in China during the Cultural Revolution and there published a newsletter entitled *The Crusader*.[25] Eldridge Cleaver, a high-ranking member of the Black Panthers, also visited China in 1969. China became central to the Black Panther's ideological development. At a meeting of radical activists, David Hilliard, a member of the Black Panther Party, declared that, "If you can't relate to China then you can't relate to the Panthers."[26] In another instance, a group of Asian-American activists asked members of the Black Panthers what they should call their newly formed organization. Bobby Seale, the chairman of the Black Panther Party, insisted that the new group call itself the Red Guard Party of America.

The relationship between China and the Black Panthers is just one example of the internationalism of the Cultural Revolution. The radicalism in China coincided perfectly with the rise of the Global Left and the general rebelliousness of the 1960s. In China, however, the global radicalism of the 1960s was presented as evidence of the importance of Mao Zedong Thought, the Cultural Revolution, and the actions of the Chinese students. Sometimes this led Chinese students and officials in the Communist Party to connect with foreign activists, as is the case of the Black Panthers. However, just as often, these students warped the events of the 1960s so that they fit a more Chinese worldview. The 1960s were therefore a powerful tool in China, as Red Guards attempted to model the Cultural Revolution for a world that seemed on the verge of revolution.

Conclusion

Much of China's global radicalism abated in the 1970s. This is especially true of foreign policy. Lin Biao's death and the threat of border wars with the Soviet Union caused China to seek an alliance with the United States.

---

25. Robert F. Williams, *Negroes with Guns* (Chicago: Third World Press, 1973).
26. *AAPA Newspaper* (March, 1969), 4; AAPA stands for the Asian American Political Alliance.

In 1972, President Nixon, the arch-nemesis of the Left, visited Beijing and met with Chairman Mao. For both Nixon and Mao, Sino-American rapprochement was a calculated political decision. Nixon, seeking re-election in the fall of 1972, believed that opening China would provide a major political boost and could potentially end the war in Vietnam. More importantly, both Nixon and Mao believed that an alliance between their two countries could serve as an important counterweight to the threat of the Soviet Union. As allies, the United States and China could work together to stave off the threat of Soviet aggression. During the student phase of the Cultural Revolution from 1966 to 1968, the prospect of international revolution was one of the central topics of the day. With American rapprochement, however, that strain of Chinese politics was greatly diminished. China had now reached a mutual understanding with the United States, a country that had been vilified only several years before. Stability replaced global revolution in Chinese politics.

The differences between the Cultural Revolution and other social movements that occurred in the 1960s in places such as France, Germany, the United States, Japan, and Mexico (to name a few) are many. For the sake of brevity we may identify four major differences between China and other student movements during the 1960s: (1) The Cultural Revolution was more violent than any other political movement during the 1960s. Even in some of the most violent moments in the 1960s, no social movement was as destructive as the Cultural Revolution. (2) The scope of the Cultural Revolution was far wider than any other political movement of the 1960s, and the tactics of the Red Guards were much harsher. Nothing was off limits, and every aspect of a person's life, including sexual history, was criticized by the Red Guards. In a decade marked by movements to create more freedom, the Red Guards effectively moved in the opposite direction. (3) There was no equivalent to the Communist Party apparatus or Mao Zedong in other countries that experienced major social movements. For one, Mao and his allies in the CCP decided when the student movement would begin and when it would end. Similarly, Mao's place in Chinese society was unprecedented. No other student group adopted such a cult-like relationship with its leader. Although Mao did not control the students' every action, each Red Guard group believed that it was effectively working for the Chairman and the party. (4) The results of the Cultural Revolution were more far-reaching than any other student movement. However, the chief outcome of the Cultural Revolution was largely unintended. After Mao's death, those who had been persecuted during the Cultural Revolution slowly returned to power. Many of these leaders turned away from radical Maoism and embraced capitalist modernization. The chaos and violence of the movement caused many to fundamentally reappraise Maoism and to search for alternatives to his brand of politics. Without the horrors of the Cultural Revolution, it is unlikely that China would have undergone such a rapid modernization, or so enthusiastically embraced capitalism.

And yet the Cultural Revolution cannot be excluded from a discussion of the 1960s. How can we even begin to link the violence and chaos of the Cultural Revolution with the Global Sixties? There seems to exist a chasm between the two. But that chasm can be closed if we avoid reducing the Cultural Revolution to a torrent of chaos and bloodshed. While not ignoring the violence of the movement, we must also recognize that student experiences during this period were varied and uneven. While some participated in violence, others expressed a sense of freedom, some of which has come out in the fiction written by former Red Guards.[27] Others found a more bucolic life in the countryside and came to admire the spirit of the peasantry. In China's cities, two of the most popular English-language titles during the Cultural Revolution were *The Catcher in the Rye* and *On the Road*.[28] The sentiments of these books, of a youthful generation seeking greater possibilities, embodied one dimension of the Red Guards, even if these possibilities were expressed through unimaginable violence. Even within this violent milieu, some students posed deeply critical and insightful questions about the state, the bureaucracy, and China's future. In Hunan, a Red Guard group wrote a series of essays that challenged the authority of the Communist Party, and accused the government of suppressing the student movement.[29] This Red Guard group, known as the *Shengwulian* (an abbreviation of "Hunan Provincial Proletarian Revolutionary Great Alliance Committee"), demanded that the government address what it saw as some of the major challenges facing China. They offered a genuine critique of Chinese society that often rose above factional politics and Maoist jargon. If anything, the *Shengwulian* and other Red Guard groups complicate the picture that the Cultural

---

27. A recent example of this fiction, available in English, is Ah Cheng, *The King of Trees: The Novellas* (New York: New Direction Books, 2010).

28. Paul Clark, *The Chinese Cultural Revolution: A History* (New York: Cambridge University Press, 2008), 228.

29. Wu Yiching, *The Cultural Revolution at the Margins: Chinese Socialism in Crisis* (Cambridge, MA: Harvard University Press, 2014).

Revolution was an orgy of violence carried out by mindless youth who were brainwashed by Mao Zedong.

Chinese youth, furthermore, connected the Cultural Revolution with the broader unrest that marked the world in the 1960s. Red Guard rhetoric was infused with references to the Civil Rights movement, the Paris uprising of 1968, and the Vietnam War. Like their counterparts around the world, they criticized racial injustice, American foreign policy, and imperialism in the Third World. However, unlike many other students, the Red Guards' understanding of the world was largely mediated through the Communist Party. These officials carefully crafted a worldview that placed China at the center of all revolutionary action. The students adopted this worldview and easily imagined that the Cultural Revolution lay at the core of the 1960s. Any protest, march, riot, or revolutionary action was viewed as indisputable proof that the Cultural Revolution was indeed a model for activists around the world. Chinese students believed the world was on the cusp of global revolution; events in Berkeley, Paris, Mexico City, Prague, and Berlin did nothing to belie this notion. In case there was any doubt about the impending revolution, the Chinese press, the Chinese Communist Party, and Mao Zedong reminded the students that the Cultural Revolution was a movement with profound global implications. The Red Guards saw themselves at the center of a vast web of activism. These international networks, both real and imagined, were what made the 1960s such a profound decade and marked a turning point in the history of the twentieth century, both in China and around the world.

Sources

Mao Speaks

"Bombard the Headquarters" is one of the most important documents from the Cultural Revolution. During the summer of 1966, as students began to rise up on college campuses and criticize school administrators and local officials, Mao remained largely silent on the particulars of the Cultural Revolution. It was left to officials like Liu Shaoqi and Deng Xiaoping to decide how to handle the students' new burst of revolutionary energy. These officials dispatched work teams to college campuses in an attempt to bring the students under the party's control. The move backfired, however, as rebellious students resisted the influence of the work teams. Because of Liu Shaoqi and Deng Xiaoping's early support for the work teams, they were accused of suppressing the students and stifling the Cultural Revolution. Although Liu Shaoqi is not mentioned directly in this document, its publication forced him to write his own self-criticism detailing all the mistakes he had made, which he presented to officials in the Communist Party. Despite Liu's ostensible contrition, he slowly lost his grip on power, and was basically placed under house arrest until his death in 1969.

Questions for Consideration

Why was the publication of Mao's article necessary? What was happening in Beijing during the fifty days before the publication of this editorial? What does the publication of this document say about the early development of the Cultural Revolution? What does the editorial's publication suggest about the relationship between Chinese students and Mao Zedong? What are the charges leveled against those who have suppressed the Cultural Revolution? Why didn't Mao accuse anyone directly in this article? Why does he only refer to his supposed enemies as "they"?

◆◆◆◆◆

"Bombard the Headquarters—My First Big Character Poster"

By Mao Zedong, *Peking Review*, August 5, 1966

China's first Marxist-Leninist big character poster and the Commentator's article on it in *Renmin Ribao* [*People's Daily*] are indeed superbly written![30] Comrades, please read them again. But in

---

30. A reference to the first big character poster, published at Beijing University on May 25, 1966.

the last fifty days or so some leading comrades from the central down to the local levels have acted in a diametrically opposite way. Adopting the reactionary stand of the bourgeoisie they have enforced a bourgeois dictatorship and struck down the surging movement of the great cultural revolution of the proletariat.[31] They have stood facts on their head and juggled black and white, encircled and suppressed revolutionaries, stifled opinions differing from their own, imposed a white terror, and felt very pleased with themselves. They have puffed up the arrogance of the bourgeoisie and deflated the morale of the proletariat. How poisonous! Viewed in connection with the Right deviation in 1962[32] and the wrong tendency of 1964,[33] which was 'Left' in form but Right in essence, shouldn't this make one wide awake?

◆◆◆◆◆

In Support of the Students

On August 18, 1966, one million Red Guards descended on Tiananmen Square to attend the first mass rally of the Cultural Revolution. This mass rally came at an important time in the Cultural Revolution. The work teams had largely been removed from college campuses, and radical students were becoming increasingly influential. The events of the day

---

31. In Karl Marx's original formulation of Communism, he postulated the core belief that the bourgeoisie, a group of mostly upper-class people that emerged in Europe in roughly the nineteenth century, needed to be overthrown in order to bring about a communist society. The bourgeoisie is essentially the enemy of the proletariat, otherwise known as the workers. Here, Mao accuses his enemies of holding a bourgeois mentality, implying that they are really dictatorial capitalists.

32. A reference to the Seven Thousand Cadres Conference, held in January 1962. At this conference, Liu Shaoqi gave a speech that criticized the policies of the Great Leap Forward, an economic campaign designed by Mao Zedong that led to widespread famine. Mao deeply resented Liu's speech and its implicit condemnation of his policies.

33. A reference to the Four Cleanups, a movement launched during the Socialist Education campaign. During the Four Cleanups, which was carried out under the leadership of Liu Shaoqi, many rural cadres were purged from the party. From Mao's point of view, the campaign was excessive and caused too much disruption in China's rural areas.

also held a symbolic importance. Between speeches, several students were invited to meet Chairman Mao. When one of the students asked Mao if he would wear a Red Guard armband, he agreed. As a result, newspapers around the country published articles like this one, reinforcing the students' importance in the Cultural Revolution. At several points, the editorial also refers to the Destroy the Four Olds campaign, a movement launched by the Communist Party. In a speech on August 18, Lin Biao ordered the Red Guards to destroy all "old ideas, old culture, old customs, and old habits" in Chinese society. The theory behind the Destroy the Four Olds campaign was that certain feudal elements had "poisoned" Chinese society and had muted the Communist revolution. If China was going to continue its progress toward a true Communist society, these vestiges of traditional Chinese culture had to be eliminated. Lin's words set off a torrent of violence, as bands of Red Guards roved the country in search of anything they thought represented "old China." In the process, the Red Guards burned or destroyed countless historical artifacts, including entire temples and ancient heirlooms.

Questions for Consideration

How does the editorial differ from "Bombard the Headquarters"? What is the overall tone of the editorial? Does this editorial tacitly sanction violence? How does the editorial's attack on traditional culture relate to the overall goal of the Cultural Revolution? What does this article say about the scope of the Cultural Revolution? What role is Mao Zedong Thought to play in the movement? Finally, while young people were not directly mentioned in "Bombard the Headquarters" they are specifically referenced here. What does this editorial suggest is the role of young people in the Cultural Revolution?

✦✦✦✦✦

"It's Fine!"

Renmin Ribao (People's Daily), editorial, August 23, 1966[34]

We hail the proletarian revolutionary rebel spirit of the young "Red Guard" fighters of Peking![35]

Chairman Mao has said: "In the last analysis, all the truths of Marxism can be summed up in one sentence: 'To rebel is justified.'"

"The Golden Monkey wrathfully swung his massive cudgel, And the jade-like firmament was cleared of dust.[36]

With Mao Tse-tung's thought as their weapon, the young "Red Guard" fighters are sweeping away the dust of all the old ideas, culture, customs and habits of the exploiting classes. Peking has been liberated for 17 years.[37] But, as a result of prolonged control and repression by the revisionist former Peking municipal Party committee, the names of many places and shops and quite a few outworn customs and bad habits in the service trades are still emitting a rotten feudal and capitalist odor and poisoning people's souls. The broad masses of the revolutionary people can no longer tolerate this.

Where the broom does not reach, the dust will not vanish of itself. Tens of thousands of "Red Guards" have wielded iron brooms and within the short space of a few days have swept away many names and customs and habits representing the ideology of the exploiting classes. This is a revolutionary action to destroy the old and establish the new. New names, new customs and new habits glittering with the proletarian revolutionary spirit,

---

34. The translation of this text can be found at http://www.morningsun.org/smash/good_indeed.html.

35. Peking is simply an older way of Romanizing Beijing.

36. From the sixteenth-century Chinese classic *Journey to the West*. One of the main characters is a mythical monkey-king, whose rebelliousness helps a traveling monk overcome numerous obstacles.

37. From 1945 to 1949, the Communists fought a civil war with the ruling Nationalist government, eventually emerging victorious. Their "liberation" of Beijing in 1949 was one of the key victories of the war.

have added boundless glory to our great capital, the centre of the proletarian revolution.

Revolutionary signs and inscriptions are everywhere. Everywhere there are revolutionary words and songs. Every street, every store and every trade must become a school for the study of Mao Tse-tung's thought and a centre for the dissemination, implementation and defense of Mao Tse-tung's thought. Mao Tse-tung's thought is illuminating every corner.

This is a great event which lifts up our hearts; a joyous event which fills our hearts with a great happiness.

The revolutionary spirit of the "Red Guards" will enable our country and people to preserve their revolutionary youth forever.

The revolutionary action of the "Red Guards" is a mighty torrent that cannot be stayed by any old conservative forces.

The proletarian revolutionary rebel spirit of the "Red Guards" is very good indeed!

◆◆◆◆◆

The Cultural Revolution and the American Civil Rights Movement

In both 1963 and 1968, Mao Zedong issued statements of support for the Civil Rights movement in the United States. In these statements, Mao claimed that the suppression of African Americans was clear evidence of the evils of American capitalism. Some radical African Americans considered Mao to be a key supporter of their movement. One such writer and activist was Robert F. Williams, an American who lived in China during the Cultural Revolution. Williams left the United States in 1961 after being falsely accused of a kidnapping in North Carolina. Williams believed that the charge was racially motivated and refused to stand trial. After spending time in Cuba, Williams came to China just as the Cultural Revolution was beginning, where, as noted above, he continued to publish a newsletter entitled *The Crusader*. He returned to the United States in 1969, and the state of North Carolina eventually dropped all charges against him. He died in 1996. Williams believed that African Americans needed to use more force in their politics, and that they had to defend themselves from violent racial attack. His ideas about civil rights and racial equality in America influenced a number of activists and organizations, including the Black Panthers. His presence in China helped the CCP and the Red Guards contextualize the Civil Rights movement, although that movement was just as often manipulated and distorted to make Mao seem more important to African Americans. All of the quotations in the article below were statements made by Williams during the summer of 1967.

Questions for Consideration

Does the article specifically discuss race in America? How does the article present the Civil Rights movement? In what ways does the author use the language of the Cultural Revolution to describe the Civil Rights movement? Is this in any way problematic? Is the Civil Rights Movement presented as equally important to the Cultural Revolution? According to the article, what was Mao's role in inspiring activists in the Civil Rights movement? Finally, what does this article suggest about the international aspects of the Cultural Revolution?

"Inspiration to the Afro-American Struggle"

Editorial, *Peking Review*, August 18, 1967

August 8 was the 4th anniversary of Chairman Mao's statement supporting the Afro-Americans in their struggle against racial discrimination by U.S. imperialism.[38] In a statement, Afro-American leader Robert F. Williams said that Chairman Mao is the first world leader to elevate the Afro-American struggle to the fold of world revolution. Inspired by Chairman Mao's statement, the Afro-American people are more and more turning to armed resistance.

---

38. Issued in 1963 at the behest of Robert F. Williams.

Williams' statement says that the nature and intensity of the present struggle of the oppressed Black people presents undeniable evidence of the impact of Mao Tse-tung's thought on the oppressed people of the world. The Afro-American people, like their oppressed brothers throughout the world, have been inspired to raise their level of struggle to a new revolutionary height.

"The phony movement of passive resistance is being thoroughly discredited and more and more the oppressed Black people are turning to armed revolutionary resistance. As the Afro-American liberation movement engulfs and enflames major American cities,[39] the Johnson Administration becomes ever more frantic and brutal in its desperate efforts to repress the heroic uprisings. It is resorting to arbitrary and vicious arrests of thousands of Black people and their leaders. It is dispatching thousands of troops armed with modern weapons of war to murder and maim the long suffering victims of fascist tyranny."

"The tide of the Afro-American freedom struggle cannot be stemmed. Johnson's savage repressive measures amount to no more than: 'lifting a rock only to drop it on one's own feet.' The flames of people's wars cannot be extinguished by tyrants."

The statement points out: "This is the era of Mao Tse-tung, the era of world revolution, and the Afro-Americans' struggle for liberation is a part of an invincible worldwide movement.... In keeping with the principles of people's war, wherein the great masses of exploited peoples of the world represent the rural masses surrounding the cities (the exploiting industrial countries), the Afro-American revolutionaries represent a mighty urban underground within the city. Our people will further develop and master people's warfare. Every battle will be a glorious monument to Chairman Mao's August 8, 1963 statement and we shall become even more fierce in resisting the tyranny of racist U.S. imperialism. We shall ever be inspired by the fact that Chairman Mao has said:

---

39. The summer of 1967 was a particularly violent moment in the Civil Rights movement. Detroit and Newark both witnessed major riots, and many activists in the movement became convinced that more direct (and sometimes violent) tactics were necessary to finally achieve a modicum of equality.

'... The evil system of colonialism and imperialism arose and throve with the enslavement of Negros and the trade in Negros, and it will surely come to its end with the complete emancipation of the Black people.'"

◆◆◆◆◆

The Red Guards in Song

Music, as in many other countries in the 1960s, played a major role in the Cultural Revolution, although its content, structure, and place in Chinese society differed greatly from that of Europe and the United States. An important difference between China and the West was that music was not made for consumption but rather to foster a revolutionary spirit and build community. During the Cultural Revolution, performing revolutionary plays and songs was an important indicator of a group or individual's enthusiasm for the movement. Red Guard groups would sing songs and put on performances to display their commitment to the Cultural Revolution, and to remind everyone of their own elite status in Chinese society. The lyrics in the song below were specifically inspired by the Communist leadership. Several lines are borrowed directly from speeches made by Communist officials. The line "we will smash the old world," for example, is lifted from a speech made by Lin Biao instructing the students to destroy all feudal culture that remained in Chinese society. Similarly, the line "dare to criticize and repudiate, dare to struggle" comes from Mao Zedong. The actual text of the song is therefore by-and-large not original, taken mostly from the rhetoric that proliferated during the Cultural Revolution. Still, one can image the powerful impact that this song had on those who were not Red Guards. As the song says, the Red Guards were the "vanguards of the Cultural Revolution."

Questions for Consideration

How does this song differ from Western pop music produced during the 1960s? Did the song below promote revolution or conformity? Was it possible to do both at once, or are these two concepts antithetical? What was the overall message of this song? What did it mean for the students to be the vanguard of the Cultural Revolution? For whom was the song intended? How do you suppose the average citizen's response to this song would be different from that of a bureaucrat or a member of the army? Finally, what does this song say about the relationship between Mao Zedong and the Red Guards?

◆◆◆◆◆

Red Guards' Battle Song[40]

We are Chairman Mao's Red Guards,
We steel our red hearts in great winds and waves.
We arm ourselves with Mao Tse-tung's thought
To sweep away all pests.

We are Chairman Mao's Red Guards,
Absolutely firm in our proletarian stand,
Marching on the revolutionary road of our forbears,
We shoulder the heavy task of our age.

We are Chairman Mao's Red Guards,
Vanguards of the cultural revolution.
We unite with the masses and together plunge into the battle
To wipe out all monsters and demons.

Refrain:
Dare to criticize and repudiate, dare to struggle,
Never stop making revolutionary rebellion.
We will smash the old world
And keep our revolutionary state red for ten thousand generations!

---

40. The translation of this text can be found at http://www.morningsun.org/smash/cr_3_1968.html (accessed April 13, 2016).

Chapter 2

Student Protests in the Black Atlantic of May 1968: Remembering Paris, Dakar, and New York

Félix Germain

By the middle of the 1960s, after having participated in the struggle to end Jim Crow and French colonialism, many African, Caribbean, and African-American students realized that the passing of the Civil Rights Act of 1964 in the United States and decolonization in the French Caribbean (1946) and former sub-Saharan African French colonies (1960) did not bring prosperity to their communities or nations.[1] Influenced by militant Black writers and activists, they yearned for a modernity that was not defined by racial inequalities, corruption, or military conflicts. They joined their counterparts around the globe in criticizing the Vietnam War and the conservative policies that many governments had enacted after World War II—but they also sought to abolish the lingering effects of Jim Crow in the United States and colonialism in the former sub-Saharan African and Caribbean French colonies.

As members of a group that has been historically misrepresented, Black students across the Atlantic were especially attuned to the cultural hegemony in their educational systems. Consequently, they considered the university as the perfect site for protest against racial inequality, neo-colonialism, authoritarian regimes, and especially European cultural and intellectual hegemony. By the late 1960s, Black students had protested at San Francisco State University in California, Cornell and Columbia Universities in New York, the Sorbonne and the Université de Nanterre in France, and the Université de Dakar in Senegal.

---

1. The French colonized many sub-Saharan African countries. The long list comprises Benin, Burkina Faso, Cameroon, Central African Republic, Chad, Republic of the Congo, Cote d'Ivoire, Gabon, Guinea, Madagascar, Mali, Mauritania, Niger, Senegal, and Togo. In the Caribbean, Haiti obtained independence from France in 1804; Martinique, Guadeloupe, and French Guiana remained French colonies until 1946, when their status changed to Overseas French Departments. This political status gave them full French citizenship.

Black students' opposition to Euro-American and French cultural hegemony took different dimensions. In Paris, French Caribbean students, who had been flirting with nationalism, asked the French government to commit more resources for development projects in Martinique, Guadeloupe, and French Guiana. They also demanded that Guadeloupean, Martinican, and French Guianese migrants in Paris be treated like their French counterparts—in other words, fairly. In Senegal, students criticized their government for being too authoritarian and demanded certain educational reforms. They wanted more financial aid and Senegalese professors, as well as a curriculum that addressed their history and social realities. In the United States, African-American students sought to enhance democratic practices throughout the country and, like their Senegalese counterparts, asked university administrators to offer courses on African and African-American experiences. As we shall see, the kind of changes Black students desired were limited and local in scope. They did not want to change the world. They merely wanted to be treated with dignity, to uplift their communities and nations, and to be represented in the process of knowledge production.

May 1968: Caribbean Migrants in Paris

In 1946, representatives from Martinique, Guadeloupe, and French Guiana signed a law that officially changed these French colonies into Overseas French Departments, or integral parts of France. By integrating into the French political system, the former French Caribbean colonies earned the right to participate in national presidential elections and to send representatives to the National Assembly and the Senate. Most French Caribbean people supported the transition from colonies to Overseas French Departments because they believed France would help decrease their poverty rates and improve their healthcare and educational systems. In many ways, this political transition represented a different type of decolonization, one premised on the fair and equal integration of the formal colonies into the "metropole."

The transition did not occur as smoothly as anticipated. Indeed, after World War II, France's economy was weaker and smaller than it had been during the interwar years. French officials now focused on rebuilding the nation and assisting the hundreds of thousands of citizens who had lost everything in the war. This meant that French

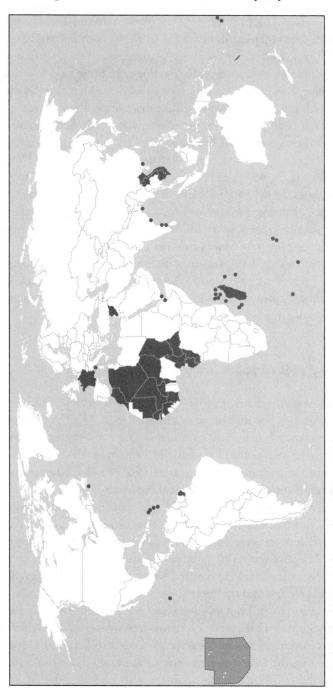

Map of the French Empire (extent from 1919 to 1939).

Caribbean people had been integrated into a relatively poor country with few resources to develop their homelands. Ultimately, by the mid-fifties, the resultant stagnant economic condition and persistent social inequalities influenced students' perception of departmentalization. The students, who had become avid consumers of anti-colonialist literature, such as *Discourse on Colonialism* (1955) by Aimé Césaire (1913–2008) and *Black Skin, White Masks* (1952) by Frantz Fanon (1925–1961), were now highlighting the gap between promises of full French citizenship and their islands' harsh socio-economic realities. Reflecting island-wide social anxieties, the students underscored the lack of professional opportunities and the growing unemployment rate. Moreover, they claimed the new political status did not preclude White French administrators from maintaining colonial relations with French Caribbean people.

But French officials ignored the students' concerns. Apparently, they did not intend to invest massively in Caribbean development projects. On the contrary, influenced by U.S. development policies in Puerto Rico, French officials sought to reduce poverty in the French Caribbean by encouraging labor migration from Martinique and Guadeloupe to France. In short, French "development strategy" aimed to improve the new Overseas Departments' socio-economic conditions by decreasing surplus labor through state-sponsored labor migration to Paris, where a plethora of jobs was available. To achieve this goal, in 1962 the French Interior Ministry created the Bureau pour le Développement des Migrations dans les Départements d'Outre-Mer (the Office for the Development of Migration from the Overseas Department—BUMIDOM), a state-sponsored organization responsible for coordinating the Caribbean migration to Paris. Many young Caribbean individuals enrolled in BUMIDOM's program, which promoted migrating to France as an entrée to a lucrative profession.

To the migrants' surprise, however, BUMIDOM only offered such underpaid, low-skilled positions as bricklayers and maids. Numerous students felt the workers had been deceived; they claimed the workers traded lives of poverty at home for lives of poverty in a cold and racist European country. In many ways, the social condition of Caribbean migrants in France was the final straw. Some Caribbean students believed the French system only worked for the French, leading the students to swell the ranks of the new nationalist parties advocating for independence. Influenced by Marxist ideals and anti-colonialist thinkers such as Fanon,[2] they wanted to control their political destiny because, allegedly, departmentalization offered zero economic benefits and promoted French culture over French Caribbean culture.

The following statement by the Organisation de la Jeunesse Anticolonialiste de la Martinique (the Anti-colonial Youth Organization of Martinique), a major nationalist organization numbering at least 10,000 students, illustrates the anger against the French government coursing through the students' veins:

> Beneath the hypocritical mask of departmentalization, Martinique is the Algeria of the past. . . . We proclaim that the status of Overseas Department clashes with French Caribbean interest and makes sustainable economic growth impossible. We want the right to industrialize and exploit our island's resources. . . . We want the right to redistribute the land and to restructure the sugar and rum factories into cooperative enterprises.[3]

In May 1968, massive protests erupted in Paris. For nearly two months, millions of French students and workers protested for educational reforms and better working conditions. Stagnant wages, students' desire for a more progressive curriculum, attractive leftist ideologies, anti-war sentiments, and a growing consciousness of the plight of the "Third World" had paved the way for what would be the largest student movement and workers' strike in French history. Students and workers took over the streets of the beautiful French capital. They chanted slogans depicting the government as a corporate puppet; they demanded that institutions serve the people, not the other way around.

French Caribbean students and workers also swarmed the streets of Paris. However, unlike the French, they fought two battles. Not only did

---

2. Frantz Fanon was from Martinique and studied in France after World War II. Trained as a psychiatrist, he wrote about the effects of French colonization on French colonial subjects. He was also a revolutionary, siding with the Algerians during the War of Independence against the French (1954–1962). By 1830, the Algerians had been conquered by an oppressive French government, and after World War II a strong nationalist movement flourished, leading to a bloody War of Independence that resulted in almost a million casualties.

3. Julien Valère Loza, *Les étudiants Martiniquais en France: Histoire de leur organisation et de leurs lutes* (The Martinique Students in France: History of Their Organization and Struggles) (Martinique: Editions 2 M, 2003), 184.

Caribbean migrants protesting with French workers, May 13, 1968. Photo A Bugat
Archives Confédérales—courtesy of the Confédération Française Démocratique du Travail.

they protest against the system with their French counterparts, they also
stood up against the policies and institutions that supposedly reduced
them to second-class citizenship. Guadeloupean, Martinican, and French
Guianese students gathered at French universities and marched on the
streets of Paris, demanding higher wages, better social benefits, and educational reforms. Additionally, they protested at BUMIDOM, asking to
reconfigure Martinique, Guadeloupe, and French Guiana's political status, as well as for better jobs for Caribbean migrants.

BUMIDOM had long been a source of anger in the community
of Caribbean students in Paris. One reason was that the organization
was entirely staffed by French citizens who not only shared a colonial
background but were also known to be extremely paternalistic toward
Black migrants. The students viewed the organization as an accomplice
of Charles de Gaulle's conservative government, which had supposedly
deceived Caribbean people by encouraging migration to France, where
a life of struggle against poverty and anti-Black racism awaited them.
Thus, in May 1968, Caribbean students, activists, workers, and nationalists took over the offices of BUMIDOM. Many students were card-
carrying communists who belonged to the Comité d'Action des

Travailleurs et Etudiants des Territoires sous Domination Coloniale Française (the Committee of Workers and Students from Territories under French Colonial Domination), a radical group founded by Caribbean students affiliated with the Sorbonne Occupation Committee. Indeed, Caribbean students had participated in the activities of the Sorbonne Occupation Committee because, as a progressive organization, the Committee believed that France was still colonizing her former colonies, including the French Caribbean Overseas Departments.

Despite being created in the heat of the moment, the Committee of Workers and Students from Territories under French Colonial Domination was well organized. Caribbean workers and students took turns occupying BUMIDOM from late May until the end of June. They prevented administrators from entering the building; some of them even vandalized the premises. In short, several grievances had fueled the protest. First, the insurgents believed the migrants, particularly women, deserved better jobs than domestics, or *filles de salle* (room attendants), a euphemism for janitors. They felt these jobs offered low wages and no avenue for professional growth. Second, they were frustrated by the various forms of anti-Black racism in Paris. Third, they asserted departmentalization was a form of neocolonization. Last, they believed labor migration was a form of exile and asked the government to help migrant workers return to their native islands.

The protests of Caribbean students and workers during the May '68 events were significant for both the migrants and the French officials in charge of supervising the migration. For one thing, it altered French officials' preconceived notions regarding Caribbean migrants. The French had historically misrepresented Caribbean people as uneducated and apathetic individuals in love with France, the irreproachable motherland. The protest, however, suggested that French Caribbean people were contentious postcolonial French citizens. Caribbean students and workers also forced French officials to re-evaluate the ways in which they integrated the migrants into the fabric of French society. Indeed, after weeks of protest at BUMIDOM, French officials made concessionary speeches, hinting that they would offer better jobs to the migrants.

Ultimately, the protests of students and workers at BUMIDOM were successful. BUMIDOM did improve the ways it integrated Caribbean migrants into the labor market. After the protests, it channeled migrants into the healthcare industry and the public sector, where they worked as nurses' aides or entry-level civil servants—steps up from the previously offered positions as hospital janitors, maids, and bricklayers. By taking over BUMIDOM's offices, the students and workers had also won a psychological victory. They encouraged French administrators to transcend colonial notions of Caribbean identity and asserted their presence as Black citizens in the French Republic. Simultaneously, the BUMIDOM takeover had a nationalistic component—it embodied the French Caribbean desire to seize control of its own destiny. This goal, however, was never realized.

That being said, the flame of nationalism did not die after 1968—if the students could not have their own country, they could still control their intellectual destiny. Thus, as Caribbean students and intellectuals returned home, they began to lay the foundations for a full-fledged university system in Martinique, Guadeloupe, and French Guiana. Eventually, in 1982, after nearly fifteen years of struggle, the Université des Antilles et de la Guyane (UAG) opened its doors to students. Reflecting the change of consciousness that occurred throughout the 1960s, UAG offered courses in "traditional" disciplines as well as the history and cultures of the Caribbean and South America.

As suggested above, the May '68 events had another meaning for Black French citizens from the Caribbean. In many ways, the struggle that took place at BUMIDOM illustrates how the transition from French colonies to Overseas French Departments was full of paradoxes. French Caribbean migrants and students had to stand up for their rights in order to secure what had been promised to them by the law of 1946, namely full-fledged citizenship and the possibility to climb up the social ladder through education and hard work. Ironically, May '68 also had an impact on other former French colonies, which had recently opted for self-rule. We shall see how this global wave of institutional, political, and cultural change affected Senegalese students.

Senegalese Students and the Protests of 1968

Historically, Senegal in West Africa had been a privileged French colony. In 1887, the four communes of Senegal (Saint-Louis, Gorée, Rufisque, and Dakar) became overseas French territories. This status granted Black African residents of the four communes (known as *originaires*, or "natives") the right to send a deputy to the French national assembly and the same municipal rights as their counterparts in France. Additionally, the colonial bureaucracy was concentrated in Dakar, where a substantial French population resided. Yet, although *originaires* of the four communes had received the same civil rights as French citizens, they remained colonial subjects. The French still argued they had a mission to civilize Senegal and the other African colonies, a pretext allowing them to exploit resources and maintain their political hegemony over much of the continent.

World War II, however, was a major turning point in French colonial history. For one thing, the German occupation had painted an unflattering image of France; it undermined France's claim to be a powerful empire capable of protecting and guiding its colonies. Moreover, after the war many strikes occurred throughout West Africa, particularly in Senegal, where, in spite of stagnating wages, labor output had been increasing due to the development of the railroad system. Similar to neighboring West African colonies, increasing popular dissatisfaction had fueled a vibrant independence movement, which also traveled to France. Indeed, by the early 1950s, Senegalese students helped found the Fédération des Etudiants d'Afrique Noir en France (the Black African Students Federation in France), a Pan-African organization promoting independence. Ultimately, by 1960, the changing geopolitical climate of the postwar period, the demands of African labor unions, and the anti-colonial activities of African intellectuals and students in Paris led to the decolonization of Senegal and the other sub-Saharan African French colonies.

But Senegal's peaceful transition from colony to sovereign nation-state did not usher in economic prosperity. Senegalese youth soon realized that French colonization had created a dysfunctional economy that rested on the fragile pillars of monoculture, notably the cultivation of peanuts. Senegalese students were also exasperated by France's influence on their society and the lack of democracy in their own country. By the mid-sixties, the decreasing price of peanuts on the world market and two consecutive droughts created the perfect conditions for social unrest at the Université de Dakar, a new university that had opened its doors in 1957. Moreover, President Léopold Senghor lost his popularity among many students. Indeed, while Senghor managed to steer Senegal away from dictatorship and authoritarianism, a problem that many West African nations faced in the 1960s, he was not totally sympathetic to the idea of a multi-party system. In fact, in 1968, Senghor was reelected in a landslide victory because the Senegalese Progressive Union, his own party, was the only one on the ballot. To make matters worse, he chose six Frenchmen for his cabinet of seventeen ministers, a move angering the students who claimed that neocolonialism structured Franco-Senegalese relations.

French influence on Senegal's national university also aroused anger among Senegalese students. The students wondered why French officials participated in the selection of the university's chancellor, deans, and directors of institutes; they wondered why so many administrators were still French when Senegal possessed its own intelligentsia. Moreover, Senegalese students claimed their university's curriculum was not adapted to contemporary African social realities. They asked why they had to fulfill the same requirements as French students to earn Senegalese diplomas. They wanted a curriculum preparing Senegalese students for the African job market. In sum, they highlighted a new problem in postcolonial Senegalese society, namely that Dakar University existed in the shadow of the French university system, a system that ironically was facing an existential crisis.

By the mid-sixties, Senegal's dire economic situation, Senghor's questionable political campaigns, the students' struggle to make ends meet, and the university administration's reluctant approach to Africanize the curriculum created the perfect climate for social protest. Senegalese university students, thirsty for an African-centered educational system, had an unprecedented desire to infuse African subjectivities into the curriculum. Yet the administration was unwilling to Africanize the university's curriculum and hire more African faculty members. Additionally, the administration offered few housing opportunities on campus, poor medical coverage, and only a handful of academic scholarships. As a result, from 1965 onward, Senegalese students began protesting for change at the university.

At first, the protests were small and sporadic. By 1968, however, led by the Union Démocratique des Etudiants Sénégalais (the Democratic Union of Senegalese Students), l'Union des Etudiants de Dakar (the Dakar Students' Union), and other students' groups composed of foreign students from neighboring African countries, the protests swept the entire university. Senegalese students were also aware of the massive student protests in France, a phenomenon that might have radicalized and encouraged them to ask for changes at the local level. On May 18, 1968, the students contacted the administration, threatening to strike if the administration decreased their scholarships and refused to diversify the curriculum and the faculty. They waited nearly ten days for a formal response. Because the administration ignored their demands, on May 27,

1968, the students went on strike. To their surprise, the events took a turn for the worse.

The police, who had earned a reputation for thuggery, surrounded the university and arrested the Senegalese and other African students participating in the strike. This latest act of institutional violence shocked Dakar's residents, who were already frustrated by the decaying economy and the rising unemployment rate. In a gesture of solidarity, they joined the students. To the government's dismay, the protests spilled into the streets of Dakar. From May 29 until June 8, Dakar was paralyzed. Students, labor union members, and unemployed citizens all voiced their anger against the unpleasant postcolonial conditions. The insurgents burned government properties, looted shops and gas stations, and threw stones at police officers. The police retaliated with their clubs, hoping to quell the protests. But, determined to win their fight for change, the protesters would not budge. Eventually, the cost of protest forced the Senegalese government to the negotiating table. The labor unions won an increase in the minimum wage, promises of curriculum reforms were made, and discussions of decreasing students' fellowships were postponed.

However, by the next academic year talks of curriculum reforms had stalled and the administration admitted fewer students. In an attempt to weaken students' leadership, the state also conscripted the most vociferous students into the military. To some extent, these tactics worked. The students' voice was not as strong as it had been in previous years. Still, student protests erupted sporadically. The quest to Africanize the curriculum and the university's faculty members channeled the students back into the streets. Ultimately, after two years of sporadic protests for diversifying the curriculum and members of the faculty, the administration finally acknowledged the students' demands. In 1971, Dakar University stopped emulating the French university system and began operating on its own terms.

May '68 in Senegal also affected the labor market and the structure of the university. The events played a major role in postcolonial Senegalese society. As Pascal Bianchini notes, the students' protest did not merely engender university reforms, it also led to the formation of new national identities.[4] For instance, after 1968, many students

---

4. Pascal Bianchini, *École et politique en Afrique noire: Sociologie des crises et des réformes du système d'enseignement au Sénégal et au Burkina Faso (1960–2000)* (School and Politics in Black Africa: The Sociology of Crises and Reforms of the Educational Saystem of Sénégal and Burkina Faso) (Paris: Karthala, 2004).

traded their French suits and ties for traditional Senegalese attire. Thus, the May '68 uprisings in Senegal signaled the beginning of a new era, one in which Senegalese people shifted their center of intellectual and cultural gravity from Paris to Dakar. This phenomenon, however, was not exclusively Senegalese. Below, we shall see how a new consciousness in Black America also engendered educational changes in the United States.

African-American Students and May '68

In 1954, the U.S. Supreme Court outlawed racial segregation in schools and other public institutions, effectively ensuring that the Fourteenth Amendment to the U.S. Constitution be applied to all citizens.[5] In the South, the decision allowed African Americans to challenge universities still denying them admission (e.g., the universities of Georgia, Alabama, Mississippi, Tennessee, and South Carolina). In the North, African Americans pressured universities to increase black enrollment. Thus, by the 1960s the presence of Black students on many campuses increased from zero or a mere handful to dozens and sometimes hundreds of students. At a time when African Americans were still struggling to obtain civil rights, the increasing number of Black students on campus changed certain universities into a hub for political activism and protest. Black students organized powerful, far-reaching organizations such as the Student Nonviolent Coordinating Committee (SNCC); they conducted sit-in protests at lunch counters throughout the South, and they rejuvenated the stalled Civil Rights Movement.

By 1966, after the passing of the Voting and Civil Rights Acts, Black student activism took another direction. Stokely Carmichael and H. Rap Brown, SNCC's leaders, broke away from the Southern Christian Leadership Conference (SCLC), the organization founded by Martin Luther King, Jr., in 1957, which played a significant role in the Civil Rights movement. Influenced by Malcolm X, Carmichael argued that

---

5. The Fourteenth Amendment states: "All persons born or naturalized in the United States, and subject to the jurisdiction thereof, are citizens of the United States and the State wherein they reside. No State shall make or enforce any law which shall abridge the privileges or immunities of citizens of the United States; nor shall any State deprive any person of life, liberty, or property, without due process of law; nor deny to any person within its jurisdiction the equal protection of the law."

King's integrationist strategy would not bring long-lasting social change for Blacks in America. He feared that in the company of too many White allies, Blacks would lose agency in their struggle for equality. For Carmichael, the "Black struggle" would be drowned in a sea of White liberalism, a sea whose currents could not lead the Black working class to the promised land. Black communities, he argued, needed economic revitalization and more political capital. Self-sufficiency and cultural pride figured high on his agenda. Carmichael summed up his political philosophy with two words—Black Power!

As the condition of Black people in U.S. inner cities worsened, Carmichael suggested that the Black liberation struggle should expand to the West Coast and Northern cities, where institutional racism also reduced African Americans to second-class citizens. His call for action appealed to a growing number of Black students on campuses who felt progress towards racial equality had stalled, as poverty, unemployment, and police brutality still affected many African Americans.[6] Carmichael's Black Power movement not only encouraged Black students to maintain close ties with their communities, but also inspired them to advocate for a new curriculum, one that would finally include the African-American experience. In short, the students wanted to uplift the Black working class and ensure that African-American subjectivities would be included in the process of knowledge creation and dissemination.

This phenomenon was clearly noticeable at Columbia University. In the spring of 1968, African-American students demanded a Black Studies program and the hiring of African-American faculty members. Demonstrating their connection to the Black community, they also criticized the administration for trying to construct a gymnasium in Harlem that would uphold Jim Crow practices by providing a separate entrance for Harlem residents, who at the time were mostly Black. In fact, criticism turned into action, as the students occupied Columbia's buildings, ultimately forcing the administration to halt the construction of the gym.

The students' fight to improve the university's relations with the African-American community bore more fruits than their quest for a

---

6. The Civil Rights Act ended discrimination based on race, color, religion, or national origin throughout the labor market and the public sector; the Voting Rights Act secured suffrage for African Americans in the South; and the Fair Housing Act banned discrimination in the sale or rental of housing.

Black Studies program. While African-American students at Columbia University forced administrators to halt the construction of the gym, they did not convince them to establish a Black Studies program. However, the fight to incorporate African-American subjectivities into the curriculum was not limited to Columbia University. By 1969, Black students were pressuring institutions such as Cornell University and San Francisco State University to establish Black Studies programs. In fact, if history remembers the spring of '68 at Columbia University for the students' protest against building the gymnasium in Morningside Park, the events that occurred at Cornell University and San Francisco State in 1969 marked the birth of Black Studies in the United States.

As was true at Columbia, students at Cornell University had been active throughout the sixties, pressing for a democratization of the university and protesting against the Vietnam War. What was different at Cornell was that its number of Black students was significantly higher than at Columbia. In 1963, Cornell had launched the Committee on Special Education Projects (COSEP), a program designed to increase the number of minority students on campus. By the standards of the 1960s, the program was highly successful; it increased the number of African-American first-year students from 8 in 1964 to 170 in the fall of 1969. Unexpectedly, perhaps, this exponential growth in Black students at Cornell, even at a time when attitudes were rapidly changing, brought swift anti-Black reactions from the campus community.

This new generation of African-American students did not believe in turning the other cheek. Influenced by Malcolm X, Carmichael, and Fanon, an intellectual who claimed violence was a means to obtaining freedom,[7] they felt entitled to being enrolled at Cornell and were prepared to struggle to assert that right. Following the burning of a cross on campus by unknown persons, in what has become one of the most memorable moments of the tumultuous sixties, on April 19, 1969, Black students and some White supporters occupied Willard Straight Hall. Strategically minded, they chose April 19 because it was on parents' weekend, therefore adding a sensational twist to the

---

7. In *Les Damnés de la Terre* (The Wretched of the Earth) (Paris: Éditions Maspéro, 1961), Fanon, discussing the impact of colonization upon natives, argued that violence against the colonizer is a necessary step toward national and intellectual liberation.

events. The students initially took over the Straight unarmed, but after White fraternity students attacked them, some students armed themselves. The takeover lasted three days and received unprecedented media attention.

Aware that the administration did not want that kind of media attention, Black students seized the opportunity to ask for a Black Studies program, which would build on the legacy of Black Nationalist leaders like Malcolm X. Cornell's administration quickly acknowledged the need to include Black experiences within the curriculum. After recruiting James Turner, a leading African-American intellectual, in the fall of 1969 Cornell University inaugurated one of the most influential Black Studies programs in the United States.

A similar story occurred at San Francisco State University (SFSU). Due to the growing number of Black students, anti-Black racism had surged on campus. But Black students at SFSU were under the spell of the Black Power movement and the Black Panther Party, which flourished across the bay. Founded in 1966 by Bobby Seale and Huey P. Newton in Oakland, the Black Panther Party sought to protect the African-American community against the frequent assaults of the Oakland Police Department. In addition to advocating for militant self-defense against police actions, they practiced a form of revolutionary socialism, which entailed the development of community programs such as shelters, schools, and food assistance programs. Thus, Black students at SFSU had also grown more radical than the previous generation of students. Undeterred by the hostile racial climate, they attended school to enjoy the fruits of equal opportunity. But they also believed in protecting themselves against White oppression, and relentlessly asked the administration to establish a Black Studies program that would contribute to the university's intellectual mission and shape the Black leaders and activists of the future.

The suspension of George Mason Murray, an English instructor and minister of education for the Black Panther Party, was the spark that ignited the fire at SFSU. Murray had allegedly told Black students to carry a weapon for protection against racist administrators. Many African-American students believed the suspension was biased; they believed it reflected the conservative and authoritarian culture plaguing their university. From November 1968 to March 1969, joined by Asian-American, Latino-American, American Indian, and Euro-American students who endorsed the idea of diversifying the university's curriculum and faculty members, African-American students went on strike. With the support of the Black Student Union, they made the following demands:

1. That all Black Studies courses being taught through various departments be immediately part of the Black Studies Department and that all the instructors in this department receive full-time pay.

2. That Dr. Hare, Chairman of the Black Studies Department, receive a full-professorship and a comparable salary according to his qualifications.

3. That there be a Department of Black Studies which will grant a Bachelor's Degree in Black Studies; that the Black Studies Department chairman, faculty and staff have the sole power to hire faculty and control and determine the destiny of its department.

4. That all unused slots for Black Students from Fall 1968 under the Special Admissions program be filled in Spring 1969.

5. That all Black students wishing so, be admitted in Fall 1969.

6. That twenty (20) full-time teaching positions be allocated to the Department of Black Studies.

7. That Dr. Helen Bedesem be replaced from the position of Financial Aid Officer and that a Black person be hired to direct it; that Third World people have the power to determine how it will be administered.

8. That no disciplinary action will be administered in any way to any students, workers, teachers, or administrators during and after the strike as a consequence of their participation in the strike.

9. That the California State College Trustees not be allowed to dissolve any Black programs on or off the San Francisco State College campus.

10. That George Murray maintain his teaching position on campus for the 1968–69 academic year.[8]

---

8. Oba T'Shaka, "Africana Studies Department History: San Francisco State University," *The Journal of Pan African Studies* 5 (2012): 21–22.

Ultimately, the students' protest at SFSU bore fruit. In 1969, the administration finally created a Department of Black Studies.

The Black students' movement to democratize and diversify the curriculum did not occur without "casualties." At SFSU, Cornell, Columbia, and various other universities, the movement was punctuated with arrests, police beatings, suspensions, and a number of threats. Yet the students prevailed. The administrators realized that establishing the programs was an investment in campus stability. Most importantly, they began to understand that teaching the history of racial minorities in the United States and abroad complemented the intellectual mission of the university. At the turn of the twenty-first century more than a hundred institutions of higher learning offer degrees in African-American Studies, Africana Studies, and Ethnic Studies. In fact, thanks to the effort and sacrifice of African-American students of the sixties, many prestigious American universities, including Harvard, Berkeley, Yale, and Northwestern University currently offer a PhD in the discipline.

Conclusion

Black students played an important role during the social and political unrest that many societies experienced during the late sixties. This chapter demonstrates how they protested in Paris, the United States, and Senegal to improve the conditions of Black workers and democratize higher education. The students of the Black Atlantic had grown more radical than in previous decades. Not only were they following in the footsteps of Black activists and intellectuals who fought against Jim Crow and colonialism, but they were also influenced by intellectuals of the postwar era like Fanon and Carmichael, who were preaching revolution and Black cultural empowerment. Consequently, cultural- nationalist motives often structured their political goals.

African-American students wanted an integral place in the intellectual infrastructure of the nation. The university curriculum, they argued, should reflect the plurality of the nation and include Black experiences. Senegalese students were on a similar quest. Indeed, Senegal had gained independence from France but unequal power relations with France persisted in the postcolonial period. The French still controlled the Senegalese government and educational system, a phenomenon that sparked protest for Africanizing the school system, empowering the working class, and claiming the Senegalese government for Senegalese citizens. In Paris, Caribbean students highlighted how regional and racial differences in the French Republic engendered social marginalization. Flirting with nationalistic ideals, they protested to improve the living and working conditions of the Caribbean diaspora in France, and upon their return to their homeland, they began laying the foundation for a French Caribbean University system. All and all, student protests in the Black Atlantic of the late sixties influenced higher education and promoted the inclusion of marginalized subjects into the fabrics of these societies.

Sources

An Iconic Image of African-American Student Protest

In the late sixties, Stokely Carmichael's call for promoting Black culture and the strengthening of Black political and economic power—in other words, his call for Black Power—gained traction among African-American students. As already noted, Frantz Fanon, the Martinican psychiatrist who urged colonized people to use violence in changing the system, also influenced African-American activists and students. Few members of the Black Panther party had not read the *Wretched of the Earth*, Fanon's magnum opus. Thus, many Black students believed that armed struggle was necessary to achieve liberation, or at best keep abusive police officers and White supremacists at bay. The takeover of Willard Straight Hall at Cornell University in April 1969 demonstrates how certain African-American students were committed to armed resistance in order to achieve social change, both on and off campus.

Questions for Consideration

As you reflect on the racial climate of the period, what do you think was the symbolic meaning of carrying a gun? Why do you think only Black males (as opposed to Black females) are seen in this photograph? Why

Cornell students exiting Willard Straight Hall led by Eric Evans, a protest leader. Office of Visual Services photographs, #4-3-2093. Division of Rare and Manuscript Collections, Cornell University Library.

do you think such forms of student radicalism were more common at San Francisco State University and throughout Northern universities than at Southern universities?

✦✦✦✦✦

Caribbean Students Discuss the Meaning of the '68 Events

The May '68 events caught Caribbean students by surprise. They were not expecting their French counterparts to stage such radical protests for an entire month. While many Caribbean students were already engaged in some form of political activism, they grabbed this opportunity to build bridges with their French counterparts, voicing their anger against the conservative Gaullist government and demanding university reforms. But they also viewed the events as an opportunity to protest against French neocolonialism in the Caribbean. Indeed, many students believed departmentalization did not serve the interests of French Caribbean people. Influenced by the wave of decolonization, which swept the former French colonies in North and sub-Saharan Africa, many students dreamt of independence or at least a different political relationship with France.

Questions for Consideration

As you read these two excerpts from *Alizé*, a French Caribbean student publication that appeared in June of 1968, reflect on the following issues. What are the connections between the student protests and the Caribbean labor migration to France? Did all Caribbean students share the same political views? Why do you think the students viewed French Caribbean people as people of the Third World?

◆ ◆ ◆ ◆ ◆

Excerpt from an Editorial Section Entitled "Action"[9]

Caribbean students and workers are deeply involved in the current events, which have brought the nation to a standstill. Although certain Caribbean people are faithful to the Gaullist government, in one form or another most of them are voicing their opposition against the system. They participate in many different ways; certain students are protesting with an unprecedented feeling of rage, while others attend the planned or spontaneous gatherings at the universities' amphitheaters. This experience is truly exhilarating!

We must also seize this moment to recognize that our societies, which have been dominated for centuries by foreigners who prioritize their interest over the material and spiritual interest of our people, are still suffering. For us, these events are exceptionally important; not only do they indicate that we must assume

---

9. *Alizé: Revue Trimestrielle Antillaise et Guyanaise D' Inspiration Chretienne (Trade Wind: A West Indian Quarterly Journal of Christian Inspiration)*, June 1968. Editorial page. No page numbers given. Translated by author.

our responsibilities, but they also represent a call for action for all men and women from the Third World.

Excerpt from "Caribbean People in the Current Social Crisis: Perspectives of Students"[10]

Caribbean people can evaluate the current events from an individual or communal perspective. But it seems that the second alternative is more logical because it provides a more global understanding of the problem. After all, Caribbean workers and students share a common history; they are a product of the colonial system; neither integrated in their own society or in France, they must constantly try to find their place in the world.

Although our society and culture differs from France, it is still modeled after French society; just take a look at our local political parties—aside from one exception, they are merely a local representation of French political parties. But the events occurring in France during the past three weeks are raising an important question, namely, what does the current crisis in France mean for the future of the Overseas French Departments? Indeed, this revolution, and we must not be afraid to utter the word, also affects French Caribbean people. For one, we are humans, and thus care about the human condition across borders and nationality. Most importantly, we are "a colonized people," and for that reason we feel much more connected to Third World countries than do people from the industrialized countries. They actually used to be colonizers. In sum, the revolution affects us because we are people—Caribbean people who want to shine.

This also means that one must understand the geographical dimension of the Caribbean experience; Caribbean people are not confined to the boundaries of their homeland, they also live in France. When analyzing the current situation one notes the following:

10. *Alizé: Revue Trimestrielle Antillaise et Guyanaise D' Inspiration Chretienne* (*Trade Wind: A West Indian Quarterly Journal of Christian Inspiration*), June 1968. Editorial page. No page numbers given. Translated by author.

1) Caribbean people in the Overseas French Departments are less affected by the crisis; they are isolated and not even aware of the chaos in the "motherland." Moreover, people in Martinique, Guadeloupe, and French Guiana only care about social development in France when it affects them; this means that they usually react after the facts.

2) Caribbean people in France face another dilemma. The rapid growth of the French Caribbean population in Paris is creating an internal colony, which has now three options; they may ignore the situation; wait and see what happen; or protest for their rights. They must choose diligently, however, because their action can shape their homeland's future.

✦✦✦✦✦

A Cartoon from the *Patriote Guadeloupéen*

Many Caribbean students were the first members of their families to attend university. For that reason, they felt quite close to Caribbean workers in Paris who came from humble backgrounds. Moreover, many of the workers were also young, usually in their early twenties. Thus, friendships between students and workers developed during cultural events and community-sponsored festivities. This connection between the students and the workers further motivated the former to present themselves as the "guardians" of the community.

The following cartoon is from the *Patriote Guadeloupéen* (The Guadeloupean Patriot), a student newsletter published in France by the Association Générale de Etudiants Guadeloupéens (the Association of Guadeloupean Students). The sentence to the right of the man states, "One of BUMIDOM's faces: A recruiting agency for French capitalists." The BUMIDOM agent holds a box with a sign: "Take advantage! Thirteen immigrants from the Overseas Departments for the price of 12 French workers."

UN DES VISAGES
DU B.U.MI.D.O.M
AGENCE DE RECRUTEMENT
POUR LES CAPITALISTES
FRANÇAIS

Le Patriote Guadeloupéen, September 1971. Le Patriote Guadeloupéen was a newsletter published by the Association Générale des Etudiants Guadeloupéens (The Comprehensive Association of Guadeloupean Students). Translated by author.

Questions for Consideration

What is the message of this cartoon? Do you think Caribbean students were merely protesting against the French or were they also influenced by a particular political ideology?

♦♦♦♦♦

A Word from the Minister of Education

In 1960, when Senegal became independent, young people felt optimistic about their nation's prospect. They imagined steady job growth in the public and private sectors, and in many ways, the new University of Dakar represented a gateway to a stimulating professional life. The transition to being a self-sufficient and successful independent nation, however, was fraught with obstacles. The economy was not diversified: a small ruling class was concentrated at the top of the social ladder, the middle class was only composed of a few workers from the public and private sectors, and many unemployed urban dwellers and peasants occupied the bottom tier of the economy. Worse, access to the university was more complicated than young people had anticipated; tuition and the cost of room and board prevented students from humble backgrounds from enrolling. Moreover, students criticized the curriculum, which they felt did not address African realities. Thus, the university became a laboratory where students questioned their leaders' allegiance to the youth and France's cultural hegemony over Senegal.

In the following document, one notes how Amadou M'ahtar M'Bow, the Minister of Education, responded to the students' protests. M'Bow's response was published in *Dakar Matin* (Dakar Morning), the most popular newspaper in Senegal.

Questions for Consideration

In reading M'Bow's response, reflect on how he defended the government. Think about how he described the students. To whom was this message really addressed? What do you think the Minister of Education tried to achieve in his address to the public?

♦♦♦♦♦

"A word from the Minister of Education Amadou M'ahtar M'bow to the students who are striking and refusing to take their exams and attending classes"[11]

Apparently, students at the University of Dakar are on strike because they wish to have more handsome fellowships, which would be paid over twelve months instead of ten. First, allow me to explain how we disburse fellowships. To be sure, our final decision is based on three criteria: the parents' income, the students' grades, and our national priorities. You can trust that our selection process is fair and elaborate, as the entrance committee over which I preside is comprised of selected government officials, professors, and members of a parent association.

---

11. *Dakar Matin*, May 27, 1968, p. 1. Translated by the author.

You shall know that for the first time in our history 600 students graduated from high school, 380 of whom were Senegalese. In 1967, when the university received a record number of applicants, we determined that we would allocate full fellowships based on grades, income, the student's disciplinary choice, and the awards won by the candidates. Obviously, due to our country's dire needs for doctors we were very supportive of pre-med students. Thus, we allocated 175 full fellowships (22,500F),[12] 129 partial fellowships (15,000F), and an additional 114 partial fellowships (11,250F). Due to the large number of fellowships that we offered, we were forced to disburse the funds over a period of ten instead of twelve months. The government was unable to offer any fellowships to foreign students.

Our university offers a state-of-the-art library and affordable room and board; a double room costs 3000F monthly and room and board is only 6,300F. Moreover, we offer free healthcare coverage. Senegalese students who started this movement do not realize that 11,250F is more money than what the average Senegalese worker earns.[13] In fact, a Senegalese peasant who has a large family often earns less than 40,000F. We should remember that in the past Senegalese students experienced much tougher conditions. Finally, we should also know that our president cares deeply about our nation; every year we find a way to send 20% of our students to study in France. Moreover, I am personally invested in the students' success. In the following month, I have scheduled a trip to Brussels, where I will ask for more fellowships in the name of our bright students. Our government, which takes education very seriously, only aspires to offer its citizens a better future.

---

12. The CFA franc, which France introduced into its West and Central African colonies in 1945, continued to be used by these nations after independence. In 1968, the hourly minimum wage for a laborer in Senegal was 48.4 francs.
13. See the previous note. A small sample of 188 workers in 1968 revealed that their average per capita annual income was 25,000 CFA francs. Each of those workers claimed to support, on average, 8.58 persons.

Chapter 3

Spring Thaw, Summer Frost: Eastern Europe in 1968

Mauricio Borrero

On August 22, 1968, the front page of the *New York Times* featured news of the invasion of Czechoslovakia by troops from the Warsaw Pact, the Soviet bloc counterpart to NATO. Overnight, Soviet troops, along with Polish, East German, Hungarian, and Bulgarian troops, had crossed the Czechoslovak borders, occupying the country and putting an end to the period of reformist Communism known as the "Prague Spring." For most of the year, the small Central European nation of Czechoslovakia had been one of the epicenters of the tumultuous events of 1968. Since January 1968, the Czechoslovak Communist Party (CzCP), under the newly installed leadership of Alexander Dubček, had begun to implement a reformist program with the goal of creating "socialism with a human face," a sharp departure from the harsh and repressive Communism of other Soviet bloc nations.

Czechoslovakia differed from other global centers of activism in 1968. In places such as France, the United States, and Mexico, the patterns of protest generally featured students and sympathizers in increasingly bitter confrontation with an entrenched political establishment. Instead, for almost eight months in 1968, Czechoslovakia became a living laboratory for the changes that could be brought by a government working in tandem with engaged, progressive sectors of the population. And whereas the limits of protest in other nations affected by the turmoil of 1968 were usually set by the governments themselves, in Czechoslovakia they were set by its neighbors, the other members of the Soviet bloc. Through the spring and summer of 1968, the Soviet Union and its other East European allies watched nervously as the pace of reforms in Czechoslovakia increased and moved in directions that they believed threatened the integrity of Communist rule in the region.

The August 1968 invasion of Czechoslovakia was in many ways an inevitable invasion, given that the Cold War had divided Europe into two ideological camps. As early as May 1968, the leaders of the Warsaw

Pact—the Communist military alliance joining the Soviet Union, East Germany, Poland, Czechoslovakia, Hungary, Romania, and Bulgaria— had been meeting to discuss invasion scenarios. For most of the summer months, observers wondered how long the Dubček government could continue its high-wire act of balancing the reformist demands of its own population with the increasingly shrill warnings from the Warsaw Pact officialdom—Communist Party leaders and newspapers—that the "Prague Spring" was going too far. When the invasion did take place, worldwide condemnation was swift and eloquent, although ultimately ineffectual. Critics of the U.S. response suggested that it was guided by the tacit acknowledgement that Czechoslovakia was part of the Soviet "backyard," and therefore not worthy of a substantial challenge beyond routine verbal condemnations. Implicit in this criticism was a critique of both superpowers—the United States and the Soviet Union—and of the two-superpower system that had taken shape in the two decades since World War II. This analysis of the global foreign policy establishment— one that equated both superpowers—was very much a part of the anti-establishment language of protests that gripped the world during 1968.

The events in Czechoslovakia—from the unfolding of the "Prague Spring," through the Warsaw Pact invasion of August 1968, and ending with the year-long process of "normalization," during which Czechoslovakia's new leaders attempted to return to pre-1968 economic and political principles and institutions—have dominated our understanding of political protest and reform in Eastern Europe in 1968. Certainly, the rise and fall of a reformist Communist government, albeit short-lived, deserves attention. But Czechoslovakia was not the only Eastern European nation that witnessed substantial anti-governmental protests during 1968. At different moments in 1968, students in Poland and Yugoslavia went on strike, occupied university buildings, and battled the police. In all three places the protests had longstanding domestic roots but were also influenced by unfolding worldwide events and the general climate of activism.

Protest and Reform in the Soviet Bloc before 1968

Although the Soviet Union and its local Communist allies ruled Eastern Europe with a firm hand, anti-governmental protests and calls for reform had been a periodic feature of these countries' political lives in the two decades since the Iron Curtain descended on the region in the late 1940s.

To understand the patterns of protest across Eastern Europe in the years leading up to 1968 it is important to disentangle four main threads of anti-governmental activism in the region. The first was provided by the economic shortcomings of the postwar Communist regimes, and found expression mostly among the working classes in protests against food shortages, strikes, and demands for better working conditions. Next, there was nationalism, specifically anti-Russian or anti-Soviet nationalism, most evident in Poland and Hungary, two nations that had suffered from Russian armed interventions over the previous centuries, most recently in 1939 and 1956, respectively. Anti-Communism was the third thread, though it came from two different sources. There was certainly and more prominently an ideological opposition to Communism itself, often driven by religious convictions, particularly in the cases of Poland and Hungary where the Catholic Church provided a strong foundation for anti-Communism, as well as parts of Czechoslovakia with its long tradition of religious nonconformism. But there were also persuasive critiques of the stifling brand of Soviet-style Communism provided by the ruling parties of the region, that were being articulated by dissenting Eastern European Communists or Marxists. Finally, there was a generational component to the protests and calls for reform, which found expression in anti-authoritarianism, critiques of the ruling establishment, and concern for the economic prospects of graduating students. This thread, more than the others, links the Eastern European protests more explicitly to other movements around the world that came to the surface in 1968.

The Soviet Union's defeat of Nazi Germany in World War II had liberated the nations of Eastern Europe from German occupation or the rule of pro-Nazi local regimes. Liberation quickly turned into occupation through the continued presence of Soviet troops and the rapid installation of Communist governments in Poland, Czechoslovakia, Hungary, Romania, Bulgaria, Yugoslavia, and Albania, as well as the Soviet zone in the eastern part of occupied Germany and the divided city of Berlin. With the creation of two rival military alliances—the U.S.-led NATO (North Atlantic Treaty Organization) and the Soviet-led Warsaw Pact—and the hardening of the division of Germany into two separate countries (East Germany and West Germany), a *pax sovietica* (Soviet peace) descended upon Eastern Europe that brought a measure of stability to a region that had suffered great human and material losses during World War II. This post-war order was built on the presence of Soviet troops, the development of a repressive internal security apparatus, and, in varying degrees across the region, a certain belief in the ideological promises of Communism.

The first challenge to this *pax sovietica* came in Yugoslavia in 1948, where the Communist leader Josip Broz "Tito" successfully resisted Joseph Stalin's attempts to bring Yugoslavia under tighter control from Moscow. Yugoslavia's ability to shake off Soviet domination was the product of specific conditions that could not be replicated elsewhere in the region. Unlike the other countries of the region, the Red Army had not liberated Yugoslavia from Nazi rule during World War II. Instead, Yugoslavia had produced its own Communist guerrilla movement led by Tito that, after a civil war with pro-royalist guerrillas, had defeated the German occupiers. Although in the late 1940s Soviet authorities condemned Tito for his deviation from ideological orthodoxy and expelled Yugoslavia from the Cominform, the international association of Soviet-leaning Communist parties, the country maintained relatively cordial relations with its Communist neighbors, especially after Stalin's death. Through the 1950s and 1960s, Yugoslav Communists experimented with ideas, such as "market socialism" and "workers' self-management," that influenced East European Communist reformers, even as the party retained its monopoly on political power.

The various cases of protest and upheaval that took place in the Soviet bloc in the 1950s had their own domestic causes. But it was not entirely coincidental that they occurred during the transition years that followed Stalin's death on March 5, 1953. After nearly three decades in power, Stalin died without a clear successor in place. For the next three months, a three-way struggle took place behind the façade of unity that the Soviet government sought to maintain. From their respective power bases in the Communist Party, the state apparatus, and the secret police, Nikita Khrushchev, Georgi Malenkov, and Lavrenti Beria uneasily shared power for the first three months until Beria was outmaneuvered by the other two and secretly executed in June 1953. It was not until 1956 that Khrushchev emerged as the dominant Soviet leader, although with far less power than Stalin. While the Soviet power struggle was unfolding, East European politics hewed closely to the zigs and zags of Soviet leadership politics.

The first major anti-government disturbance within the Soviet bloc took place in East Berlin in June 1953. Against a tense backdrop of increased emigration to the West, harassment and repression of youth organizations, and poor living standards, the East German government approved a set of measures that included higher taxes, higher prices, and an increase in the productivity quotas required of workers. On June 16, several hundred construction workers went on strike to protest an announced pay cut. The strikers gained the support of other workers and a general strike was called for the next day. Overnight the number of protesters swelled to almost 25,000. As demonstrator demands escalated to include the resignation of the government, Soviet troops assisted East German police in violently suppressing the protests. Estimates of the dead were in the hundreds, and over 5,000 individuals were arrested and sentenced to labor camps.

The speech that Khrushchev gave behind closed doors to selected delegates at the end of the Twentieth Congress of the Soviet Communist Party (CPSU) in February 1956 has generally been seen as the marker of his emergence as the uncontested leader of the Soviet Union. In what came to be known as the "Secret Speech," Khrushchev presented a forceful and passionate, albeit selective, denunciation of the "cult of personality" that Stalin had built over his years in power, and also the arbitrary persecution of Soviet and foreign Communists in the 1930s during the period of the Great Purges. In denouncing Stalin, Khrushchev was ostensibly trying to shift the blame for Communism's failings onto one man and his allies, while preserving the validity of the Communist project itself.

The reverberations of the "Secret Speech" were soon felt across Eastern Europe, where hardline Communist leaders had modeled themselves as "little Stalins" and now found their Soviet patrons moving to initiate rather than obstruct reforms. But Khrushchev's reformism was anything but consistent, and events in Poland and Hungary in 1956 would soon show the limits of the Soviet commitment to reform. A few months after Khrushchev's speech, on June 28, 1956, workers in the Polish industrial city of Poznań took to the streets. By the late morning, almost 100,000 workers had congregated near Adam Mickiewicz Square in the city's downtown, demanding better salaries and lower food prices. As tensions increased on the square, home to the city's Communist Party and government offices, elements in the crowd turned to violence, storming a nearby prison and attacking the Communist Party headquarters. When local troops failed to restore order, the national army and Soviet troops were brought in. Two days later, the protests had been quelled.

The handling of the Poznań protests exacerbated internal divisions within the Polish Communist leadership that dated to the 1940s. By

In 1968, Poland's sixty-three-year-old Wladisław Gomulka—seen here with Leonid Brezhnev to his left. Brezhnev, then the General Secretary of the Central Committee of the Communist Party of the Soviet Union—was closing in on twelve years in power. (CC by 3.0 U.S.)

October 1956, the divisions were out in the open and the Central Committee of the party moved to appoint Wladisław Gomulka as its General Secretary, despite opposition from Moscow. Khrushchev himself flew to Warsaw to persuade the Polish leadership not to appoint Gomulka, but his plane was kept from landing until the Central Committee had finished its voting and declared Gomulka its new leader. This challenge to Moscow's authority in the region was eventually papered over as Gomulka proved willing to work within the parameters of relative autonomy set by Moscow.

A far more direct challenge to Soviet dominance in the region came in Hungary, within a few days of the "Polish October." In July 1956 Mátyás Rákosi, Hungary's ruler since 1945, was forced to resign. Although Rákosi was first succeeded by another hardliner, Ernö Gerö, the change in leadership opened the political arena to more reformist Communists as well as students and intellectuals. Through the late summer and fall, students and journalists became more active through student circles and public forums, where Hungary's current problems were discussed more openly, and in October Gerö gave way to Imre Nagy, a Communist with reformist credentials who had been jailed by Rákosi.

As Hungarian students and activists developed an increasingly broader program of political reforms that challenged the Communist Party's political monopoly and questioned Hungary's international alliances, the situation quickly unraveled beyond Nagy's control. By November 1956, Khrushchev ordered Soviet troops into Hungary, and installed a more pliant government. Resistance to the Soviet troops was fierce and bloody, but ultimately unsuccessful. Although the Soviet Union was able to maintain its control, the suppression of the Hungarian Revolution of 1956 greatly affected its international prestige, particularly within the Western European Communist movement and among left-leaning artists and intellectuals, who were not entirely comfortable with the stifling nature of Soviet Communism. To the extent that the New Left was not sympathetic to Soviet-style Communism in 1968, the invasion of Hungary had helped set the tone.

Even the Soviet Union, the bulwark of Communist power, could not escape this pattern of political unrest and attempted reforms. Historians are still uncovering the full history of the period, but one major disturbance stands out from this time: the June 1962 riots in the southern Russian city of Novocherkassk. As with earlier instances of protest in the Soviet bloc, the Novocherkassk riots were set in motion by the government's doubling of the prices of basic necessities, such as bread and butter, coupled with an increase in the production quotas required of workers. Thousands of workers from the Novocherkassk Electric Locomotive Works marched on the city center, only to be met by the bullets of Soviet army troops. Close to twenty workers were killed, almost one hundred were wounded, and seven were given a death sentence and executed.

By 1964, Khrushchev was losing the support of senior Soviet Communist leaders. Citing "hare-brained schemes," such as his impulsive bureaucratic reorganizations and the foreign policy adventurism that led to the Cuban Missile Crisis in 1962, the Politburo removed Khrushchev from power in October 1964 and replaced him with the less unpredictable Leonid Brezhnev. Although Brezhnev's long rule (he stayed in power until his death in 1982) is now identified with stagnation, cronyism, and corruption, the early years hinted at a more cautious but steady reformism than that of his predecessor. His prime minister, Aleksei Kosygin, put forward a plan to increase the autonomy of state-owned economic enterprises with the goal of increasing their performance. The tentative "Kosygin reforms" were diluted by the opposition of entrenched bureaucratic interests, and by 1967, the Soviet reformist impulse, mild as it had been, had stalled.

Living in societies where information was censored or partially distributed, the Eastern European protagonists of 1968 were unlikely to be well informed about these incidents of protest and reform. News of major events like the Polish October or the Hungarian Revolution certainly spread by word of mouth or via the broadcasts of foreign stations like the BBC World Service, Voice of America, and Radio Free Europe. But lesser-known yet massive provincial disturbances, such as the 1956 Poznań protests or the 1962 Novocherkassk riots, remained unknown until the late 1980s. Even the contents of Khrushchev's Secret Speech, widely known in the West, were not fully revealed to the Soviet public until the *glasnost* years of Mikhail Gorbachev.

But the Communist Party leaders of Eastern Europe were well aware of their countries' recent history. Their response to the protests and attempted reforms of 1968 was shaped by the instability that lay not too far beneath the harsh reality of Communist dictatorship. It was also the response of established leaders, who had either been in power for many years or whose image personified old age and resistance to change in a year where youth made a confrontational stand. In this the Communist leaders were not too different from some of their Western counterparts, such as Charles de Gaulle in France, Gustavo Díaz Ordaz in Mexico, and Francisco Franco in Spain, a country that also witnessed widespread student protests against a dictatorial regime that had been in power since 1939. In 1968, Poland's sixty-three-year-old Władisław Gomulka was closing in on twelve years in power, while Bulgaria's fifty-seven-year-old Todor Zhivkov had ruled since 1954. East Germany's Walter Ulbricht, perhaps the most ardent opponent of the Prague Spring among the Eastern European leadership, was seventy-five and had been in power since 1950. The soon-to-be-deposed Antonin Novotný of Czechoslovakia was sixty-four and had been in power since 1953. At fifty-six, Hungary's János Kádár, who had been installed in power by Soviet tanks in 1956, was one of the two youngest Warsaw Pact leaders, next to Romania's fifty-year old Nicolae Ceaucescu, who had only been in power since 1965 and who refused to join in the invasion of Czechoslovakia. Even Tito, well-regarded by the Western press and openly courted by Western leaders as a wedge in the Communist movement, was in the eighth decade of his life, and had been in power for twenty-three years by the time of the events of 1968.

Polish Prelude

In 1968, the opening challenge to the established order in the Soviet bloc took place in Poland on the campus grounds of the University of Warsaw. On January 15, the Polish government announced that within two weeks it would close down the Polish National Theater's performance of the poetic drama *Dziady* (Forefathers' Eve). Written by the revered nineteenth-century author Adam Mickiewicz, *Dziady* occupied a prominent place in the Romantic era and the Polish literary canon, harking to the years when Poland had been partitioned by its neighbors and disappeared as an independent state. The complicated play embraced themes of love, death, and folk morality, but it was the nationalist themes celebrating the struggle of Polish political prisoners under Russian Tsarist rule that most resonated with Polish audiences. The anti-Russian message was not explicitly anti-Communist, and the play had been performed numerous times in the past, before the Polish authorities inexplicably decided to close it down. On January 30, 1968, three hundred students met to protest the forced closing of *Dziady*. The government's violent response to the protest triggered a wave of protests and turmoil across the country that continued through the early spring of 1968.

It was not surprising that the opening salvo of 1968 in the Soviet bloc took place in Poland given its long history of contentious relations with the Russian Empire and the Soviet Union. Despite the mantle of Communist orthodoxy imposed by the Soviet Union, nationalist undercurrents were never far from the surface in Polish political discourse. In the two decades since World War II, the Soviet leadership had developed a looser way of dealing with Poland that allowed for several diversions from the more orthodox model imposed elsewhere, most notably with regard to the Polish Catholic Church and the absence of collectivized agriculture. It also allowed for a greater degree of cultural liberalism that recognized the longstanding bridges between Polish and Western European cultures, especially in literature and the arts. By the 1960s, writers and intellectuals were reasserting themselves publicly, coming together around the issue of intellectual freedom and censorship. In March 1964, for example, writers and academics, known as the "Group of 34," published a letter protesting the government's censorship policies.

A more powerful intellectual challenge, in the eyes of the Communist leadership, came from within the ranks of the party itself. In the autumn of 1964, two graduate students and Communist Party members, Jacek

Kuroń and Karol Modzelewski, wrote an open letter to the Polish Communist Party in which they analyzed from a Marxist perspective the existing political situation in the Soviet bloc. Kuroń and Modzelewski argued that a gap had developed between the working classes of those countries and the ruling "central political bureaucracy." Following Marxist principles, they concluded that eventually that gap or conflict would lead to revolutions in Eastern Europe. They were arrested in March 1965 and imprisoned for three years. Censored inside Poland, the Kuroń/Modzelewski critique found a broader audience outside its borders, and was widely circulated among radical French students in the turbulent month of May 1968. The letter also introduced Western socialist audiences to the Polish situation, so that when student protests broke out in March 1968 they were well covered by the European press, especially the French press.

The pace of protests in Poland picked up in March 1968. On March 8, a small student demonstration within the University of Warsaw campus was met by a larger contingent of "workers' militia," who chased and beat the students while police officers watched and arrested the fleeing students. The following day, in response to the unprovoked attack on the students, close to 20,000 students marched through the city center, where they too were met by violence from police officers. Street battles between students and police continued for the next few days and spread to other Polish cities such as Kraków, Gdańsk, Poznań, and Łódź.

The Polish government's response to the student protests was similar to that of other besieged governments in 1968: violent repression on the street and harsh condemnation in the press. The Communist Party newspaper *Trybuna Ludu* led the charge in trying to exploit the student/worker divide by portraying the students as pampered beneficiaries of the state's generosity, who were now turning against it. In this there were similarities to other hot spots of 1968, such as France, Senegal, Mexico, and the United States. But there was a darker subtext that emerged in the Polish government's response to the protests: a willful manipulation of anti-Semitic currents in Polish society by singling out Polish Jewish students as responsible for the protests and labeling them agents of "international Zionism." A virulent anti-Semitic campaign followed, directed at students and party leaders of Jewish background. Whether or not the campaign was part of broader political machinations of the Minister of the Interior, Mieczyslaw Moczar, the result was that in a few short months, Poland's centuries-old Jewish community, already decimated by the Nazi wartime genocide, further dwindled to about 1,000, as Jews left the country of their own volition or with the government's encouragement. By late March, the Polish government had succeeded in shutting down the student movement. The University of Warsaw bore the brunt of the ensuing repression with eight departments closed, thirty-four students expelled, and 1,000 students forced to reapply for admission. Although the context of the Polish protests was unique to the country and its position inside the Soviet bloc, the language and methods of the Polish students' protest was similar to that of other students around the world. And yet for all its importance in the unfolding of events in 1968, the Polish protests were limited to the world of students. By late March 1968, far more momentous changes were taking place elsewhere in the Soviet bloc, and Polish students were aware of them. In statements and slogans of the protesting students, such as "Poland awaits its Dubček," there was also the awareness of and support for the changes that were already unfolding in neighboring Czechoslovakia, where a reticent reformist Communist, Alexander Dubček, had been recently appointed General Secretary of the Czechoslovak Communist Party.

The Prague Spring

The period that has gone down in history as the "Prague Spring" was the product of a series of factors: leadership changes at the top level of the Czechoslovak Communist Party; a number of domestic political, cultural, and economic issues that were impacted by the leadership changes; steady pressure from neighboring Warsaw Pact countries on the new leadership; and the impact on the Czech situation of the international climate of protest and activism that shaped the year 1968.

Czechoslovakia, along with more peripheral Bulgaria, was one of the countries where Soviet rule had not yet been outwardly challenged. To its more contentious neighbors, Hungary and Poland, the Czechs appeared "docile" and willing to accept their place in the Soviet order. Czechoslovakia had in fact been the only Eastern European country where the Communist Party had come to power through an, albeit suspect, electoral mechanism. By the early 1950s it too had its own Stalin-like leader in Antonin Novotny, General Secretary of the Czechoslovak Communist Party.

But Czechoslovakia had its own historical traditions that shaped its Communist experience and that, as events came to a head in 1968, would make the Prague Spring an event of greater historical impact than events in the other Eastern European nations. Czechoslovakia had come into existence after World War I, patched together from three historical regions of the old Habsburg Empire, Bohemia, Moravia, and Slovakia. Bohemia and Moravia were predominantly ethnic-Czech regions that had been among the most vibrant in the Habsburg Empire. Bohemia in particular, with its capital in Prague, had a long industrial tradition with an assertive working class. Unlike its neighbors, Czechoslovakia could point to a substantial democratic experience in the interwar period, before the country became a victim of Nazi expansionism in the late 1930s. The region also had a long history of contacts with the Western world, and in the first half of the twentieth century, Prague had emerged as a major Central European intellectual and cultural center. Czech students and intellectuals were very much in tune with Western currents, even the countercultural ones that surfaced in the 1960s. As recently as 1965, the American Beat poet Allen Ginsberg had visited Prague, invited to conduct poetry readings by students from the city's prestigious Charles University. In his two months in Prague, Ginsberg managed to be arrested three times for unruly behavior, and was elected King of May by the Charles University students at their unofficial May festival, which led to his deportation one week later.

Ginsberg's visit to Prague did not occur in a vacuum. By the mid to late 1960s, youth in Czechoslovakia, like many of their counterparts across Eastern Europe, were very much in tune with the youth culture that was transforming Western societies. The Soviet bloc had developed its own networks of underground youth clubs, rock bands, and counterculture, which Communist officials tried to suppress or coopt, not always with success. In their acceptance of blue jeans, rock 'n' roll, long hair and beards, and other symbols of Western youth culture, Soviet bloc youth signaled that it shared the values of this new global youth culture. Yet, as polls showed during 1968, the Czechoslovaks' acceptance of Western cultural products, particularly its youth culture, did not necessarily translate into an acceptance of capitalism. The main impetus behind the Prague Spring was not to supplant Communism but to reform it, by democratizing decision making, allowing greater freedom of expression, and improving its economic performance.

By 1967, the government of Antonin Novotny, who had ruled Czechoslovakia since 1953, had run into substantial opposition both inside the

Czechoslovak Communist Party (CzCP) and the population at large. A reformist faction within the Communist Party was gaining influence and power. While visiting Moscow in the summer of 1967, the Czech party activist Zdenek Mlynar told an old student friend from Moscow State University by the name of Mikhail Gorbachev that Novotny was rapidly losing his authority. A few months later Mlynar was appointed to the Central Committee of the CzCP. From this position he would go on to play an important role during the Prague Spring, including being one of the authors of the famous "Action Program of the Central Committee of the Czechoslovak Communist Party," which became a blueprint for students and Communist reformers elsewhere in Eastern Europe. (See the sources at the end of the chapter.) Throughout the fall of 1967 tensions within the Communist Party pitting reformers against conservatives came to a head, while students from Charles University clashed with police in October 1967. In December the Soviet leader Leonid Brezhnev visited Prague in an attempt to mediate between the two factions. His subsequent refusal to directly endorse Novotny's failing leadership was the green light that Communist Party reformers needed to make their grab for power.

Novotny's fall came in two stages. On January 5, 1968, he was replaced by Alexander Dubček as First Secretary of the Communist Party, but retained his post as president of Czechoslovakia. In a one-party state, following Soviet precedent, the former post was far more influential. With Dubček in charge of the Communist Party, the reformers began to advance their agenda, often in tandem with other influential members of the Czech public: writers, journalists, academics, and students. For the next two months, until forced to resign as president in March 1968, Novotny and his allies embarked on a rearguard public criticism of Dubček and the reformists through speeches at workplaces and factories.

The centerpiece of the Prague Spring was the Action Program of the Central Committee of the Czechoslovak Communist Party, drafted in the early months of 1968, and unanimously adopted by the Steering Committee of the Communist Party in March and by the Central Committee of the party in April. The Action Program reaffirmed Communism as its goal and Czechoslovakia's alliances with the Soviet Union and the other Warsaw Pact nations, but it altered the road map to Communism by advocating a new model for socialism that was democratic and unique to Czechoslovak conditions. Responding to the demands of Slovak party activists who had long resented the domination of the Czechs in

Czechoslovakia, the Program called for a new federalist model to accommodate the interests of both nationalities. In the political sphere, the Program rejected the Stalinist model of Communism, with its excessive intrusion into citizens' lives and its reliance on fear and terror to enforce conformity, promising instead freedom of the press, freedom of assembly, freedom of religion, and the rehabilitation of political prisoners.

Within this framework, the main events of the Prague Spring unfolded in rapid succession. The first strikes since the Communist takeover in 1948 took place in March 1968. Previously taboo topics such as the political purges of the early 1950s and the fate of political prisoners were discussed openly by the Communist Party and in the press. In late March 1968, 3,000 victims of early purges met in Prague to demand justice. The Communist newspaper *Rudé Právo* (Red Truth) became a leading advocate of the reforms, speaking out against censorship, criticizing Novotny, adopting a new language that deemphasized the importance of the class struggle in advancing Communism, and publishing exposés of Soviet secret police activities in the late 1940s and 1950s. Even the Catholic Church benefited from this political opening, and in mid-April representatives of the Vatican came to meet with Czechoslovak authorities to discuss issues of religious freedom. One month later, three Catholic bishops who had been expelled in 1948 were allowed to return to Czechoslovakia.

Students were active participants in this process, supporting Dubček, demonstrating against Novotny while he was still in power, and holding "teach-ins," very much like their Western counterparts. Across the nation, they formed clubs and groups that defined themselves as apolitical—a far cry from the tight control that Communist parties across the region had sought over students and youth. The lecture halls of Charles University and other universities continued to serve as meeting places for the multiple discussions that took place during these months. Students were also not afraid to enter the domain of foreign policy, protesting the knee-jerk anti-Americanism of the government media or marching toward the Polish Embassy in Prague to protest the rising tide of Polish anti-Semitism and the suppression of the Polish student movement.

Yugoslav Interlude

While the events in Warsaw and Prague were well-known and publicized around the world, events in a third Eastern European Communist capital received far less publicity. On June 2, 1968, a series of disturbances broke out in Belgrade, Yugoslavia (now in present-day Serbia) as a result of security personnel's refusal to allow students into a concert for members of the Communist Youth Organization in the city's suburb of New Belgrade. The standoff quickly turned violent as police opened fire on the students and the students seized a police water cannon, which they drove through the surrounding neighborhoods. A student action committee was quickly formed and organized a demonstration for the following day in front of the parliament building in downtown Belgrade to protest police violence. After this demonstration was met with further violence, close to 10,000 students occupied the nearby campus of the University of Belgrade, launching a strike that lasted one week.

Although the strike was triggered by the violent response of the police on June 2 and 3, the previous years had witnessed the gradual development of an anti-establishmentarian outlook that was not much different from that which had inspired student activism elsewhere in the world. The Belgrade students resented the government's authoritarianism, were concerned about recently implemented economic reforms and their own employment prospects, and were in solidarity with global youth issues of the day, such as opposition to the Vietnam War.

Since breaking with the Soviet Union in 1948, Yugoslavia had followed a distinctive brand of Communism, which differed substantially from the highly centralized, ideologically rigid Soviet model that had also been imposed on the rest of the Soviet bloc. The basic features of the Yugoslav model were formulated in April 1958 at the Seventh Congress of the League of Communists of Yugoslavia (LCY), the official name of the Yugoslav Communist Party. These included the ideas of "workers' self-management," "socialist democracy," "federalism," and at the international level, "non-alignment," an independent path between the two Cold War superpowers. Five years later a new constitution proclaimed Yugoslavia a "socialist federative republic," whose citizens had the right to self-management.

Yugoslavia's willingness to experiment with some features of Communism, made it an early center for relatively more candid intellectual and theoretical discussions about Communism. As in Poland, there was a small but influential group of Marxist academics who provided a forum for criticizing the shortcomings of the government. At best, they were tolerated, but as long as they were working within the ideological boundaries of Communism, they were not persecuted or banned. Much of this discussion took place in the pages of the magazine *Praxis*, first published in October 1964 with an editorial board drawn primarily from the universities of Belgrade and Zagreb. The magazine played an important role in shaping the Yugoslav student movement of the mid and late 1960s. With the publication in 1965 of an international edition of the magazine in English, French, and German, the influence of *Praxis* extended beyond Yugoslavia's borders. Its international advisory board included leading Western Marxist thinkers of the time. From 1963 to 1974, Yugoslavia was also home to a summer school in the Adriatic island of Korčula that attracted leading Marxist intellectuals from the East and West as its faculty.

As the world around them became more radicalized in the first half of 1968, Yugoslav students followed suit. Since autumn 1966, the Yugoslav Student League (YSL), the student arm of the LCY, had organized street protests against the Vietnam War in major Yugoslav cities, some of which were met by violence from the police. In January 1968, a more critical editorial board took over the weekly newspaper *Student* in Belgrade, a change that was echoed by other student publications in Zagreb, Sarajevo, and Ljubljana. Two months later, the YSL's organization in the Philosophy Faculty of the University of Belgrade agreed to a call for "new activism." This was one of the two departments of the university that would play a leading role in the June strike.

Students and their representatives were concerned about domestic issues. Delegates to the YSL conference of May 11–12 called for better conditions at Yugoslav universities and for greater democratization of university life, and they also called for concrete steps to reduce the unemployment that had risen as a result of the 1964 economic reforms. But students were also in tune with the events taking place elsewhere in these turbulent months. In April 1968, over the objections of the leadership of the YSL and LCY, sociology students at the University of Belgrade collected fifteen hundred signatures for a letter expressing solidarity with the Polish students' "struggle for the democratization" of Poland. The letter also criticized the anti-Semitic campaign unleashed by the Polish Communist Party leadership. In May 1968 several hundred students protested the emergency laws that the West German parliament was about to adopt by staging a sit-in at the West German embassy.

This was the context for the student strike that broke out on June 3, 1968. By the following day students and some university professors in Zagreb, Ljubljana, and Sarajevo had come out in support of the Belgrade students and started their own protests. Over the next few days students and professors sharpened their message, calling for greater political freedoms and greater social equality, while denouncing the party leadership and their allies as the new "red bourgeoisie." The striking students received the support of the Belgrade liberal intelligentsia, most notably the film director Dušan Makaveyev, the poet Desanka Maksimović, and university professors such as the Marxist philosopher Mihailo Marković. Some Belgrade factory workers sent delegations to the university to show their support of the students. Just as the strike was gaining support from larger sectors of Yugoslav society and the party leadership was considering the necessity to call in the army to put down the strike, Tito's deft political maneuvering stole the initiative from the students.

On June 9, Tito appeared on national television and gave verbal support to the students' demands, threatening to resign if a way was not found to meet them. Most of the students, with the exception of those in the Faculties of Sociology and Philosophy, returned to class. The students' apparent victory was short-lived. On June 26, speaking at the congress of the Trade Union Federation, Tito singled out "extremist voices" in the journal *Praxis* as responsible for the recent protests, thereby signaling the beginning of the backlash. Almost a month later, on July 19, the LCY expelled the party organizations of the Philosophy and Sociology Faculties of the University of Belgrade in reprisal for supporting the strike. The repression that followed was in line with that of the Yugoslav state in this period: not excessive or heavy-handed but efficient enough to disperse the movement and discourage further protests.

In their scope and repercussions, the events at the University of Belgrade had far less international impact than the events in Warsaw and Prague. Ironically, despite its greater openness to Western Marxist currents and the presence of a significant number of Yugoslav seasonal workers in countries such as West Germany and Sweden, Yugoslavia had its own unique makeup—a multi-ethnic federative republic that shaped the outcomes of its student movement. The Yugoslav student movement remained active after the suppression of the June 1968 protests. Student strikes and protests continued through the mid-1970s. The symbolic end to the era of student protests came in 1974 with the government's closing of *Praxis*, followed by the expulsion of eight professors from Belgrade University who were associated with the journal.

An Invasion Foretold

It did not take long after the fall of Novotny and the rise of Dubček for outside opposition to the new direction of Czechoslovak Communism to manifest itself. While the outside world welcomed the Czech experiment in creating "socialism with a human face," the Soviet bloc leaders were not comfortable with it. Their unease can be traced at several levels: bilateral meetings between individual leaders and the new Czech leadership; joint Warsaw Pact meetings that sometimes included Czechoslovakia and sometimes did not; increasingly hostile editorials from Communist Party–controlled newspapers; and military maneuvers by Warsaw Pact forces in or near Czech soil. It is difficult to pinpoint the moment when the Soviet leaders and their Warsaw Pact allies made the decision to invade Czechoslovakia, but from the flurry of diplomatic meetings and newspaper editorial invective it is clear that from the early stages of the Prague Spring, the Warsaw Pact leaders were already very concerned about its possible outcome. In a year of widespread turbulence that received ample international coverage, the Czech political process was never a purely domestic one.

The record shows that the Czechoslovak leaders, particularly Dubček, met frequently with their Eastern European counterparts in the first half of 1968. Naturally, relations with the Soviet Union were foremost in importance. The strongest show of support came from Tito in Yugoslavia and Ceaucescu in Romania. Dubček also seems to have met most frequently with the Hungarian leader János Kádár, the most reluctant of the would-be invaders. The most critical comments came from East Germany, Poland, and, of course, the Soviet Union. As usual, the Bulgarian leader Todor Zhivkov kept a low profile. Relations with the Polish leader, Gomulka, were more strained, in great part because the Czech leaders and press commented frequently on the difficult Polish situation of March and April 1968, condemning the anti-Semitic turn that the Polish crisis took.

The Warsaw Pact leaders met frequently as a group. Although the Czechoslovak situation was not on the agenda at the March meeting of the Warsaw Pact in Sofia, Bulgaria, it became the dominant issue at subsequent meetings. The earliest sign of open hostility toward the Czech experiment came at a meeting of the "Five" (the Soviet Union, East Germany, Hungary, Poland, and Bulgaria) and Czechoslovakia, held in Dresden on March 23, 1968, one week after Poland had expelled

The showdown came on the night of August 20/21, 1968, when massive numbers of Warsaw Pact troops crossed over the borders of Czechoslovakia. (CC by 3.0 U.S.)

Czechoslovak journalists for their critical coverage of the Polish student protests. The Soviet, Polish, and East German delegations took the lead in criticizing Dubček and his policies, using the damning term "counterrevolution" to describe the situation in Czechoslovakia. Two months later at a Warsaw Pact meeting in Moscow that did not include Czechoslovakia, Brezhnev continued the attack on the Dubček government, arguing that Czechoslovakia's economic reforms were only paving the way for the reestablishment of capitalism. Four days later, on May 8, the "Five," meeting again without the presence of the Czechs, discussed plans for the invasion of Czechoslovakia. The following day, the Warsaw Pact began military maneuvers along Czechoslovakia's borders with Poland and East Germany.

Tensions between Czechoslovakia and its Warsaw Pact allies escalated through the summer of 1968. As reforms kept gaining momentum, Dubček found it increasingly difficult to both slow them down and to convince the Soviet Union and its allies that he could control the pace and direction of reforms. It was particularly difficult for the Communist Party to channel the process of political democratization. In late June, the Czechoslovak parliament approved laws that rehabilitated the victims of political trials. Widespread support for a multi-party system, a logical consequence of the democratization process, brought the Communist reformers against one of the cardinal elements of Soviet-style Communism: the leading role of the Communist Party. The months of June and July witnessed increasingly hectic meetings between the Czechoslovak leadership and the other Warsaw Pact nations. The meetings took place against a background of Warsaw Pact military maneuvers and strident newspaper editorials against Czechoslovakia from other Warsaw Pact newspapers. While the decision to invade was not taken lightly, by early August it was becoming increasingly clear that the two sides—the Czechoslovak leaders with the support of most of their population and the Warsaw Pact hardliners, notably Poland and East Germany and ultimately the Soviet Union—were heading toward a final face-off. That showdown came on the night of August 20/21, 1968, when massive numbers of Warsaw Pact troops crossed over the borders of Czechoslovakia.

The Aftermath of Eastern Europe's 1968

In the long run, the most visible consequence of 1968 in the Soviet bloc was the defeat of the notion that Communist governments could implement far-reaching structural reforms. The Soviet Union led the way, as the Brezhnev government finally shed whatever mild reformist inclinations it had considered in the years between 1965 and 1967, settling instead for a long period of "stagnation," that lasted at least until Brezhnev's death in 1982. The other Communist parties of the region became increasingly ossified, dominated by careerists or status quo politicians, and hostile to reformers. By the early 1980s, it was not an exaggeration to refer to the leadership of the Soviet bloc nations as "gerontocracies"—oligarchies ruled by old men—and the annual photographs of the May Day parades in Moscow gave irrefutable visual proof of the aging leadership. While the Communist leadership held on to its monopoly of power, it lost its monopoly on the possibility of reform, which it had held in 1968. Thus, when a true Communist reformist came to power in the Soviet Union in 1985, he did not have any East European allies with whom to work.

Internationally, Soviet-style Communism was further discredited. In the short run, the invasion of Czechoslovakia gave rise to the notion of the "Brezhnev Doctrine," which stated that the survival of a Communist government was the concern not only of that nation's government, but of all other Soviet bloc nations. Implicitly, it meant that the Soviet Union reserved the right to intervene in other Soviet bloc nations if it considered it necessary.

The invasion of Czechoslovakia was followed by a year-long period in which the reformist measures of the Prague Spring were steadily dismantled, culminating in the appointment of Gustav Husak as General Secretary of the Czechoslovak Communist Party (CzCP) in September 1969. During the next two decades, under the banner of "normalization," the Husak government emerged as one of the most reactionary in Eastern Europe. However, "normalization" was not able to completely silence opposition voices, only push them underground. The 1976 arrest and trial of the members of a popular psychedelic rock band, the Plastic People of the Universe, led to the drafting of a document that helped coalesce various strands of continued opposition to the government. Known as "Charter 77," the document powerfully articulated a vision of human and civil rights that later provided a common platform of action when the Communist government fell in 1989.

Normalization was also the order of the day in East Germany and Bulgaria, while Romania in some ways moved "back into the future," as its long-term leader, Nicolae Ceaucescu, increasingly adopted some of the traits associated with the personality cult of Joseph Stalin from the 1930s to the 1950s. Ironically, it was Hungary, the country that had suffered the invasion of Soviet tanks in 1956, that provided a minor exception to the lack of reform in the region. There, Janos Kadar, who had been installed by the Soviets in 1956, quietly presided over a program of limited economic reforms that allowed for some free market elements. Known to some as "goulash Communism," Kadar's program gained him the grudging respect of segments of the Hungarian population.

In Poland, the revolutionary situation that the Polish Marxist Kuroń and Modzelewski had foreseen continued to ripen behind the façade of normalization, although in ways they may not have visualized. The 1970s were a decade of renewed labor activism, capped by the election in 1978 of a Polish cardinal as Pope John Paul II of the Roman Catholic Church, an event that provided a great boost to Poland's religiously infused nationalism. After repeated conflicts and strikes in 1970 and 1976, in the fall of 1980 the workers of the Lenin Shipyards in the port of Gdańsk went on strike, giving birth to *Solidarnosc* (Solidarity), the first independent trade union in the Communist world. For the next year, as Solidarity—with the crucial support of the Catholic Church—flexed its muscles in a new political landscape, Polish and international observers wondered whether the Soviet Union would once again invoke the Brezhnev doctrine and invade Poland to put an end to this deviation from the principles of Soviet-style Communism. But in December 1981, instead of a Soviet-bloc invasion, the Polish Army declared martial law, outlawed Solidarity, and imprisoned its leaders. The Polish "normalization" of Communist rule under General Wojciech Jaruzelski differed from Czechoslovakia's in two main ways. Solidarity proved a more resilient adversary with broader support among the Polish population, and with the rise of Mikhail Gorbachev to power after 1985, the Soviet Union was no longer a reliable opponent of reforms.

Twenty-one years after the disappointments of 1968, Eastern Europe had its successful revolutionary year in 1989. In rapid succession, and in remarkably nonviolent fashion, the region's Communist governments fell like the proverbial dominos that had once provided such powerful imagery for Western anti-Communist containment policies. In April 1989, Solidarity was again legalized and allowed to take part in the parliamentary elections scheduled for June of that year. The Solidarity candidates won the overwhelming majority of the vote and assumed power in September 1989. In October 1989, Hungary's Communist Party dissolved itself, renamed itself the Hungarian Socialist Party, and introduced legislation that created a multi-party democratic system. In East Germany and Bulgaria, Soviet pressure helped convince the leadership to give up power in November 1989. Only in Romania, where Ceaucescu and his wife were executed on Christmas Day by an army-backed National Salvation Front that had turned against the government, was there a violent transfer of power. Two years later, in 1991, Yugoslavia once again proved to be the exception, as the multi-ethnic federation imploded in a bloody civil war that brought back many of the horrors of ethnic cleansing and genocide that Europeans thought had been left behind in 1945.

To the extent that the disappointments of 1968 laid the ground for the successful revolutions of 1989, it was Czechoslovakia that once again provided the most powerful set of symbols. A peaceful student demonstration in Prague on November 17, 1989, started the chain of events that would lead to the Communist Party's announcement eleven days later that it would give up power. On December 10, the same Gustav Husak who had been installed by the Soviet leadership as Communist Party leader in 1969, resigned after appointing the country's first non-Communist government in four decades. Two weeks later, the same Alexander Dubček who had become the face of the Prague Spring, was appointed speaker of the new federal parliament, an honorary but profoundly symbolic gesture. Appropriately enough, Czechoslovakia's nonviolent revolution came to be known as the "Velvet revolution," a name that would not have been out of place in 1968, and Václav Havel (1936–2011), a playwright and poet who had become politically active during the Prague Spring and been persecuted in its aftermath, after signing Charter 77, became the first president of post-Communist Czechoslovakia.

The different ways in which the events of 1968 unfolded in Eastern Europe suggest that despite the Soviet Union's attempt to cover the region with a blanket of Communist uniformity, the Soviet bloc was anything but a monolith. The patterns of protest in March 1968 in Poland were in many ways closer to those in the West: student protests on university campuses followed by violent government suppression. The summer events in Yugoslavia differed only in the nuances provided by a savvier popular leader, Tito, and a less overtly repressive Communist government. It was in Czechoslovakia that a more distinctive pattern of protest developed, with the Dubček government serving as a vehicle for reform rather than an obstacle. For a few heady months, until a foreign invasion put an end to the experiment, the vision of a government working with its population to improve society captured the imagination of the world.

Sources

Appeals and Resolutions of Polish students in Warsaw, March 1968

Like their counterparts in Western Europe and the United States, Polish students spoke out forcefully against their government's abuses of power. They also sought to link their ideas and demands to the broader spectrum of Polish society. The two documents excerpted below show both sides of their collective voice. The first, a resolution by students from the University of Warsaw, is a direct and forceful condemnation of the use of force by police on their campus. The second is a much broader appeal by students from the Technical University of Warsaw to the Polish citizenry, presenting the students' version of recent confrontations with the police.

Questions for Consideration

What were the Warsaw students protesting against in these two documents? What vision of society comes through in their letters? How does the students' use of language compare to that seen in the other two documents presented in this section? In what ways were the concerns and demands of Polish students part of the global patterns of student protest rather than protests against Soviet-style Communism?

✦✦✦✦✦

March 11, 1968, Warsaw. Resolution of students from the University of Warsaw, condemning the brutal actions taken by police and security forces, demanding the punishment of agents representing the authorities who are guilty in violating rights.[1]

We, the students, gathered on March 11, 1968, in the Main Auditorium of the University of Warsaw, moved and shocked by the developments, which recently took place on university grounds and on the streets of our city, declare:

The current situation on the grounds of Warsaw universities is a result of the violation of fundamental democratic civil liberties, and the breaking of basic human rights and principles of societal life.

WE ARE PROTESTING

against disruption of the rule of law, against the violation of the PRL Constitution, against the interference in the lives of students by the security forces, against the brutal actions taken against students by the uniformed police and civil authorities, against all efforts to spread feuds in the Polish nation, in particular against

---

1. Zygmunt Hemmerling and Marek Nadolski, eds., *Opozycja wobec rzadow kommunistycznych w Polsce, 1956–1976; Wybor dokumentov,* (Warsaw: Uniwersytet Warszawski Institut Nauk Politycznych, 1991), 301–3. Translated by Jacek Czarnecki.

any attempt in creating a resonance between the working class and the students, we condemn any display of anti-Semitism.

WE PRONOUNCE

that the student conduct in the University gathering on March 8, 1968, was controlled and prudent. We condemn the Warsaw press for their attempts at portraying the activities in universities as if conducted by empty-headed youth and hoodlums.

WE ASK

1. Who called in the paramilitary forces that showed up on March 8, 1968, in front of the University of Warsaw dormitories even before the beginning of the student gathering?
2. Who allowed paramilitary forces to enter university grounds armed with batons?
3. Who bears the responsibility for the brutal actions by the police?
4. Who is the author of the articles, which falsified the events and were printed by the Warsaw press?

WE DEMAND

1. Full reinstatement of student academic rights for those taken away from the University by the Minister of Education, a decision that was not based on proper regulations, as well as remit all steps taken in repression, which are kept hidden by the Disciplinary Commission for political reasons. The removed students, who are dealt with by repression and about whom the press distributes fraudulent information, are our friends and members of our academic fellowship.
2. Immediate release of all students and academic researchers, detained and arrested in the latest action by the authorities.
3. Immediate and harsh punishment of those policemen and paramilitary troops who entered university grounds.
4. A complete compensation for [the] physical and moral violation against victims.
5. For the press to immediately correct the falsified reporting of the events and the publication of the names of people, responsible for the initiation of the repression against the students

6. The assurance of [an] institutional guarantee of obeying the principles of academic freedom and learning.

We demand the return of our freedom to defend ourselves against disciplinary actions, and the return of open trials. We demand autonomy to a certain degree for all higher education institutions.

With the utmost deliberation we fulfill and will continue to fulfill [the] academic obligation that rests upon us. We will not betray the trust of the nation; we will defend freedom and all who fell victim to socialism.

We direct the present declaration towards the university authorities in Sejm, Chairman of the board of ministers of PRL, to the Minister of Education, and the Warsaw press.

The above declaration has been adopted in the presence of the Senate and mass of gathered academic researchers. The declaration was voted upon by about three thousand students with one vote against and one vote abstaining from.

◆◆◆◆◆

March 21, 1968, the students of the Technical University of Warsaw appealed to the nation, explaining the demonstrations in the academic circles, demanding from the state authorities an objective report on the student movement.

AN APPEAL TO THE CITIZENS OF THE PEOPLE'S REPUBLIC OF POLAND[2]

We, the students of the Technical University of Warsaw University, gathered during a two-day occupational strike, hereby present our stand in the following document on the March events.

We are proud that the students from our university have shown in their demonstration the uncompromising will to fight

---

2. Ibid., 314–15.

against lies, hypocrisy, and distortion, to defy brutality and the reign of vicious laws in our nation, and have shown sensitivity on national matters as well as declaring patriotic feelings and loyalty to the socialist ideologies. Despite the fact that the latest events flared passions, no one ever used anti-systemic, anti-Soviet, or anti-national phrases . . . However, the official version about alleged instigators recruited from unidentified so-called "politically bankrupt" circles and their influence on the minds of the youth are to us primitive, demagogic lies.

. . . We are demonstrating against the violations of the law that confiscate and censor letters sent by students from Warsaw, and gestures such as calling to active military duty students deemed "dangerous," revisions in universities, etc.

In regards to our petition we are not alone. Among those, who know our chants and demands, the overwhelming majority are people of good will—they are with us.

Long Live Poland!
Long Live Socialism!
Warsaw, March 21, 1968
Students from Technical University of Warsaw

✦✦✦✦✦

Action Program of the Central Committee of the Czechoslovak Communist Party, April 1968

On April 10, 1968, the Central Committee of the Czechoslovak Communist Party adopted an "Action Program," the most frequently cited example of the new political course it sought to chart for the country. The Action Program outlined a plan of political and economic reforms in a wide range of areas, and occupied a central place in the sequence of rapidly unfolding events that became known as the Prague Spring. The excerpt below highlights four major areas where the Communist Party sought to make lasting changes in Czechoslovak political and economic life: the role of the Communist Party in Czechoslovak society, the foundations of a new socialist democracy, the role of independent enterprises in a Communist society, and the guidelines for the country's foreign policy.

Questions for Consideration

Who are the various audiences that the Central Committee is addressing in this document? What is the vision that the Central Committee is laying out in this document? Would you say the Central Committee is charting a bold new path or trying to conduct a balancing act? Where in the document do you see evidence of political compromise among various interests inside and outside of the party?

✦✦✦✦✦

The Leading Role of the Party: A Guarantee of Socialist Progress[3]

[Introductory sections deleted.]

At present it is most important that the party adopt a policy fully justifying its leading role in society. We believe this is a condition for the socialist development of the country....

In the past, the leading role of the party was usually conceived of as a monopolistic concentration of power in the hands of party organs. This concept corresponded with the false thesis that the party is the instrument of the dictatorship of the proletariat. That harmful conception weakened the initiative and responsibility of the state, economic, and social institutions, damaged the party's authority, and prevented it from carrying out its real functions. The party's goal is not to become a universal "caretaker" of society, bind all its organizations, and watch every step taken in fulfillment of its directives. Its mission instead is primarily to inspire socialist initiative, to demonstrate

---

3. Jaromir Navratil, ed., *The Prague Spring 1968: A National Security Archive Documents Reader* (Budapest: Central European Press, 1998), 92–95.

communist perspectives, their modes, and win over all workers by systematic persuasion and the personal examples of communists. This determines the conceptual side of party activity. Party organs should not deal with all problems; they should encourage others and suggest solutions to the most important difficulties. But at the same time the party cannot turn into an organization that influences society by its ideas and programs alone. It must develop through its members and bodies the practical organizational methods of a political force in society....

As a representative of the most progressive section of society—and therefore the representative of the prospective aims of society—the party cannot represent the full range of social interests. The National Front, the political force of the manifold interests of society, expresses the unity of social strata, interest groups, and of nations and nationalities in this society. The party does not want to and will not take the place of social organizations; on the contrary, it must ensure that their initiative and political responsibility for the unity of society are revived and can flourish. The role of the party is to find a way of satisfying the various interests without jeopardizing the interests of society as a whole, and promoting those interests and creating new progressive ones. The party's policy must not lead non-communists to feel that their rights and freedom are limited by the role of the party....

✦✦✦✦✦

Fritz Behrendt, "A Blow against Imperialism," 1968

Condemnation beyond the Soviet bloc of the Warsaw Pact invasion of Czechoslovakia was widespread and vociferous, particularly in newspaper editorials and cartoons worldwide. One example, below, comes from the pen of the renowned German-born, Dutch cartoonist, Fritz Behrendt (1925–2008). Over a caption that reads (in translation), "A Blow against Imperialism," Behrendt drew a landscape of destruction with the ruined remains of structures labeled "Stalinism" and "Terror," and gravestones labeled "Berlin" and "Budapest," in reference to the Soviet military interventions that put down worker's strikes in Berlin in 1953 and the

"Een slag tegen het imperialisme." Fritz Behrendt, *Waakzaams en steets paraat: Navo en Warschau Pakt in karikatuur* (Amsterdam: Van Soeren, 1994).

Hungarian national revolution of 1956. A military boot is ruthlessly crushing the only sign of life in the entire landscape, a flower with the face of Alexander Dubček and leaves that read, "Communism with a human face."

Questions for Consideration

What is the message that Behrendt tries to convey in this political cartoon? Given the experience of Communism in Eastern Europe, does he oversimplify or has he captured an essential truth about the invasion of Czechoslovakia? Is Dubček an accurate or appropriate symbol of the Prague Spring, or should it have been represented differently? What emotions does the cartoon convey? How well do these emotions represent popular responses to the invasion?

Chapter 4

Mexico's 1968 Olympic Dream[1]

Elaine Carey

In 1968, Mexico appeared immune to the multiple social and political problems that plagued the United States and France. Having finally emerged from a decade-long Revolution (1910–1921) and the subsequent years of nation-building, Mexico experienced an economic miracle beginning in the 1930s, and now, in the 1960s, the country seemed on its way up. Young Mexicans were flocking to the universities, the government debated lowering the voting age from 21 to 18, and the country was mobilized to host the XIX Olympiad, *El Año de la Paz* (The Year of Peace). Mexico was to become the first Spanish-speaking (and developing) country to host the Olympics, and significant innovations in technology and communication would help broadcast the event around the globe—the major U.S. television networks would devote roughly as much news time to the Olympics as they did to the Vietnam War—providing Mexico with an unprecedented amount of media exposure, and showcasing the country as a shining example of progress and modernity in the "Third World." Appearing peaceful, progressive, and modern, the country was ready for its moment on the global stage.

President Gustavo Díaz Ordaz expressed concern at the expenses likely to be generated by hosting such an international event. In anticipation of the country's moment in the global spotlight, Mexican officials undertook massive construction projects and subsidized artistic endeavors in order to commemorate the hosting of the games and to glorify the power of the ruling party. Stadiums, hotels, and apartment buildings now dotted the Mexico City landscape, and the new subway system connected the hotels to the historic district. Prominent architects built elaborate sporting venues, and Mexico's most famous artists decorated the

1. This chapter draws on material in my book *Plaza of Sacrifices: Gender, Power, and Terror in 1968 Mexico.* (Albuquerque: University of New Mexico Press, 2005). Excerpts used with the permission of the publisher. I would like to thank Raúl Álvarez Garín, Sandra Peña, Marcelino Perelló, Lucía Rayas Velasco, and José Agustín Román Gaspar.

facades of the new structures. To overcome the stereotypes of the "sleepy Mexican" and the "land of *mañana*," Mexicans became consummate hosts and hostesses to any major fiesta. Mexican Olympic Chairman Ramírez Vazquez worked with various groups to stage dances, art exhibitions, and competitions in order to showcase the many facets of Mexican culture.

But the Mexican government's carefully constructed image of the country as content and peaceful collapsed when violence erupted in the streets in late July 1968, just as the Olympic time trials began. Street fighting between secondary-level students evolved into a massive social movement led by university and high school students that challenged the Mexican government and its historical past. The student movements that emerged during the 1968 Olympics permanently altered the nation. Though many historians have held that the 1968 Mexican student movement was simply part of a generational conflict, it was actually a far more complex social movement featuring an array of actors jockeying to define its course and its future.

The Eruption

The global celebration of Mexican modernity fell prey to localized demands that very summer. Mexican students had organized protests against the government for much of the first half of the twentieth century, and student politics had long been confrontational. The future leaders of the ruling party were plucked from the ranks of the victors in battles between student factions. Students had long protested increases in fees and poor working conditions for medical students, and struggled to gain representation in university governance. Different factions in the ruling party employed thugs to keep the students under control and sway their politics. In 1968, the ability of these older men of the establishment to control student politics suddenly collapsed when the students looked beyond their limited protests of university issues and organized into a mass movement attempting to tackle much bigger social issues.

The movement began when two student protests that reflected the different backgrounds and ideologies of the protesters met in the old section of Mexico City. On July 26, the Federación Nacional de Estudiantes Técnicos (National Federation of Technical Students; FNET) planned a demonstration to protest police violence against the students at vocational schools affiliated with the Instituto Politécnico Nacional (National

Polytechnic Institute; IPN, or Poli). The activists in FNET held close ties to IPN, vocational students, and the Secretariat of Public Education (SEP). The FNET march ultimately wound from a campus to Mexico City's main square, the Plaza of the Constitution (better known as the Zócalo). Meanwhile, in the south of Mexico City, groups affiliated with the Universidad Nacional Autonóma de México (National Autonomous University of Mexico; UNAM) also prepared to march.

Whereas Poli was home to students from families of the emerging middle class and had the mission of educating technicians, UNAM, as Latin America's oldest (it was founded in 1551), largest, and best university, was home to Mexico's intellectual, academic, and social elites. UNAM, as an autonomous university, received state funding, but it had its own governing structure. The president of Mexico appointed the rector (president) of UNAM, and he held tremendous power not only within the university but also within the ruling party, Partido Revolucionario Institucional (Party of the Institutional Revolution; PRI), and the nation. Despite their significant differences, these two student groups shared some commonalities. Like their global counterparts, they protested the war in Vietnam, studied the teachings of Mao, listened to and played rock and folk music, and saw themselves as part of an increasingly global movement that would bring change to their country.

The UNAM students, who were commemorating the fifteenth anniversary of Fidel Castro's attack on the Moncada Barracks on July 26, 1953—the event that triggered the Cuban Revolution—were also demonstrating against the United States' involvement in Vietnam. The two groups, numbering approximately 5,000 protesters in aggregate, met in the streets surrounding the main plaza.

As the two demonstrations merged, street fighting broke out between the students and the 200 *granaderos* (riot police) stationed in the area to maintain control. Student activists and passersby fled into the surrounding streets and shops. In a radio interview, Mario Ortega Olivares recalled that upon his entering the Zócalo, the *granaderos* arrived and began to beat the students. Ortega said, "A granadero arrived and gave me a club to the head and I left running. Thankfully, the people in the shops in the area protected us ... someone put me in an elevator and later we fled after the police had left to attack our comrades."[2] The protection of activists

---

2. Mario Ortega Olivares, interview, transcript in *1968, El fuego de la esperanza*, by Raúl Jardón (México, D.F.: Siglo Veintiuno Editores, 1998), 148.

and students by non-protestors, which continued throughout the movement, reflected a distrust of the government and its forces.

Three days of intense fighting followed the July 26 clash, culminating in a police and Army rocket attack on a high school affiliated with UNAM on July 28–29. After blasting open the baroque doors of the San Idelfonso campus, the military and *granaderos* entered the school. They reported that they detained 126 young men and confiscated ten molotov cocktails (gasoline-filled bottles with a cloth fuse), two cans of gasoline, a five-liter bottle of nitric acid, a bottle of ammonia, and a box of propaganda from the Partido Comunista de México (Mexican Communist Party; PCM).

These assaults by soldiers and police, which resulted in a number of student deaths and injuries, ignited student outrage against the government's actions. On the morning of July 30 and continuing through August 1, military and police units occupied areas surrounding preparatory and vocational schools. The presence of armed forces around these schools contributed to further outbreaks of violence, and numerous students were injured or killed by the soldiers and police.

After the attack on San Ildefonso, students began to organize themselves specifically to combat the government's use of force. They also sought to end the occupation of their schools and the campaign of disinformation being waged in the press by the government that portrayed them as communists, foreign agents, or both. The students also demanded that the Mexican government serve the people, and—more provocatively—they began to reclaim their own schools.

Young men and women set out to build a movement that differed from previous student uprisings by organizing across institutions and across Mexico City. More importantly, they directly challenged the Mexican government's authority. First, students organized *guardias*, comprised of eight to ten unarmed students who volunteered to remain in school buildings during the night. They hoped that the physical presence of these *guardias* would deter police or military occupation. Meanwhile, other student groups provided support and assistance. They sent food and supplies or simply offered their moral support to those occupying the schools.

Both young men and women joined the *guardias*, which meant sleeping at the school without parental supervision, a requirement that some found problematic. The presence of members of the opposite sex in close, unsupervised proximity to one another created difficulties for young women from "good" families, and clashed with cultural expectations about a young woman's behavior and capabilities. Carmen Landa, a student activist whom this author interviewed in 1996, stated that the young men in the *guardia* at her school simply assumed that women would not join. Her parents and her male comrades at her secondary school rebuffed her initial efforts to become a member of the *guardia*. She continued to press her desire to join, finally gaining acceptance from her male peers because she was the only student who knew how to operate a mimeograph machine. Because she would only teach other students to use the machine in exchange for a position with the *guardia*, she was grudgingly admitted.[3] Regardless of such problems, the young men and women, such as Carmen Landa, who joined the guardias and Comités de Lucha (Committees of Struggle) laid the infrastructure for the movement.

In the days following the San Ildefonso incident, the movement heated up. As young men and women formed informal associations, such as the *guardias*, in response to the fighting, students from IPN and UNAM, two otherwise competing campuses, aligned themselves with one another as well as with the students from the National Agricultural School and the National Teacher's School. In public meetings, students addressed the issues they thought they needed to resolve immediately. Students from various schools gathered at Poli in the summer of 1968 and formulated their first set of demands.

From these initial assemblies, they released their demands on August 1, 1968. The demands included respect for democratic liberty; the expulsion of certain police officials from their positions; disbandment of the *granaderos*; an indemnity for the families of injured or dead students; release of all student prisoners; and abolition of Article 145 of the Penal Code (an article of sedition).[4] These demands would become the basis of the "Six Point Petition" (as it later came to be known) that circulated later in September. Along with the demands, students opted for a city-wide student strike. The strike swept across the city and spread to the provinces, where students protested in solidarity with their urban counterparts.

---

3. Carmen Landa, interview with author, October 21, 1996, Mexico City.
4. The demands were published in several newspapers. See *El Universal*, July 30, 1968; and *El Día*, July 30, 1968.

The Movement

With nascent strike and student organizations at various campuses already in place, students from across the city elected representatives for a Consejo Nacional de Huelga (National Strike Council, CNH), which formed on August 8, 1968, to oversee the city-wide strike and serve as a leadership body for the movement. As with the *guardias*, both men and women served on the CNH, but it still mirrored Mexican society in that young men dominated. Only 10 of about 230 elected members of the CNH were women, according to the estimate of member Adriana Corona.[5] In a few cases, women represented schools and departments that were predominantly male. The CNH also selected members to engage in negotiations with the government as representatives of all the students involved in the strike.

Despite the fact that only about 230 people had been elected, Corona further estimated that there might have been upward of 500 activists affiliated with the CNH, a number that included representation from the provinces.[6] Corona's estimates rely upon the fact that at CNH meetings and events, council members were accompanied by friends or lovers who worked on the strike and in the movement. Other activists worked with the CNH distributing information supplied by student organizations, labor, and the Left.

The CNH and the student movement as a whole were ideologically diverse. Students identified themselves as Marxists, Socialists, Trotsky-ites, Guevaristas, and Maoists.[7] Others saw themselves as more moderate or even conservative and aligned with the right-of-center opposition party, the Partido Acción Nación (National Action Party; PAN). Other students held ties to the reigning PRI, which had continuously held power in Mexico since 1929 (although its name had changed several times). Though many right-wing students joined the protests, the majority of politically conservative students were found in those student organizations that opposed the student movement. These students also organized to protest. Right-leaning students voiced the fear that the presence of radical and leftist students in the protest movement might lead to a

---

5. Jardón, *1968: El fuego de la esperanza*, 297.
6. Ibid.
7. Guevaristas drew their inspiration from the Cuban Revolution and one of its key figures, the Argentine-Cuban revolutionary Ernesto "Che" Guevara (1928–1967).

communist or socialist revolution. In some cases, they infiltrated the leftist student movement or fought those students in the streets. Some students who disagreed with the strike and the movement fled to universities outside of Mexico City in nearby states such as Puebla and Hidalgo, while other students wished only to pursue their education, and still others grew increasingly afraid of the increased militarization of their campuses and the internal struggles between students. Moreover, certain students worked for the Olympic committee serving as translators and cultural ambassadors.

The organization of the council ensured that it included a diverse range of student voices. Students had to be elected to the council by their school or department, and the Committees of Struggle of the various schools and departments facilitated the voting for representatives on the CNH. The Committees were the initial promoters of the movement, and activists in them were responsible for organizing on the campuses and disseminating the ideas and programs of the Committees. The council was therefore an umbrella organization that developed after the movement emerged. By holding elections for the CNH, students who might not have otherwise been selected won elections because they mobilized support from their colleges. Eloquent rhetoric was also a factor that helped determine who was elected. A few female representatives were elected from fields of study that had been traditionally dominated by men such as law. Representatives elected to the council from certain professional schools also tended to be less radical than members from other schools.

New "lightning brigades" were extremely effective at promoting the political and social ideals of the movement. Initially ad hoc in their formation, these brigades were usually composed of six to ten students and included both young men and women, just as in the *guardias*. Some of the lightning brigades were organized according to the members' particular skills: for example, there were medical and legal brigades. Other brigades were formed by the Committees of Struggle with the sole purpose of spreading the message of the movement within particular schools and departments. When the CNH and the different committees issued statements, the brigades took to the streets to spread ideas and to organize solidarity, often traveling around the city via commandeered buses. Upon arriving at a site, the brigades would stand in major intersections. At times they simply passed out their flyers in the intersection. If a driver was not willing to take a flyer, the students often tried to push it through an open car window. Other times, students addressed people in a public area, reading the demands of the movement or discussing the issues. Some students did not find such literature and tactics to be effective, and adopted more creative ways to spread the message. They wrote slogans on walls and painted and printed posters that criticized or sought to humiliate the government, *granaderos*, and President Díaz Ordaz. The lightning brigades would take on a new and more defined role during the August 13 march in which thousands participated.

A few short days after the lightning brigades were formed, the CNH directed them to spread the Six Point Petition and to demand public dialogue between government representatives and the movement.[8] The Six Point Petition, first developed in the early days of the movement at Poli, ultimately read:

1. Liberty for all Political Prisoners.
2. Dismissal of police chiefs General Luis Cueto Ramírez, Raúl Mendiolea, and Armando Frías.
3. Abolition of the corps of granaderos, direct instruments of repression, and the prohibition of similar corps.
4. Abolition of Article 145 of the Penal Code [which provided for juridical instruments of repression].
5. Indemnification of the families of the dead and injured who had been victims of the aggression since July 26.
6. Determination of the responsibility of individual government officials implicated in the bloodshed.[9]

The petition reflected the students' desire to create a modern, liberal nation in which the ideals of the Constitution of 1917 were respected. The constitution, a revolutionary document that guaranteed civil rights and liberties, emerged from the Mexican Revolution. The students

8. Consejo Nacional de Huelga, "Al pueblo de México, a los estudiantes, maestros, y padres, de familia," *El Día*, August 16, 1968, also published in Ramirez, *El movimiento estudantil* (México, D.F.: Ediciones Era, 1969), 95.

9. Donald Mabry, *The Mexican University and the State: Student Conflicts, 1910–1971* (College Station, TX: Texas A&M Press, 1982), 252; and Elena Poniatowska, *Massacre in Mexico*, translated by Helen R. Lane (Columbia, MO: University of Missouri Press, 1975), 53. The FNET issued demands on July 26 that called for the firing of police chiefs and indemnification. After the march on August 1, 1968, students from Poli and UNAM demanded the abolition of Article 145 and *granaderos*, release of student prisoners, and respect for democratic liberties, as well as indemnification and firing of police chiefs. The release of all activists arrested was expanded to include all political prisoners.

The August 27 March. Photo courtesy of Marcelino Perelló, personal files.

argued that the government violated those guaranteed rights. Along with respect for the law, students wanted the government to accept responsibility for its use of repressive measures. On August 27, newspapers carried announcements inviting all the Mexican people to join the popular demonstration in defense of democratic liberties to take place beginning at the National Museum of Anthropology and History at 4:00 in the afternoon; the demonstration and march would end in the Plaza of the

Constitution—the Zócalo. Many accepted the invitation. By 2:15 p.m., buses from UNAM and IPN arrived at the museum transporting student activists; by 4:00 p.m., eighty-seven different groups were lined up for the march. These included students, teachers, the Coalition of Parents and Teachers, workers, people from the provinces, and street vendors. From 400,000 to 500,000 individual protesters also took the activists up on their invitation and joined the march. The August 27 march demonstrated that the movement had a mass appeal that went far beyond the young students.

Students, organized by schools or academic departments, carried placards with images of Mexican independence and revolutionary leaders. Reporters commented that upon passing the U.S. Embassy, the students yelled "Assassins! Assassins!" and "Cuba si, yanquis no!" (Cuba, yes! Yankees, no!)[10] By 6:35 p.m., the first wave of demonstrators entered the Zócalo, where they found that activists had created a stage out of parked IPN buses. For many of the students, it was a giant outdoor party. By 7:30, the cathedral in the plaza was aglow with lights, and the students rang the bells as the demonstrators gathered. Speakers followed one after another on the stage, discussing the student demands. Though most students dispersed after two hours, between 3,000 to 4,000 students and teachers continued to occupy the plaza. At 9:45 p.m., the students still in the plaza raised a red and black flag of revolution alongside the Mexican flag. Symbolically, the raising of the flag signified that they had taken the plaza. The festive atmosphere ended when the department of the Federal District used bullhorns to announce that the students were in violation of the law, and that they had five minutes to vacate the plaza before they were forcibly removed. At approximately 1:00 a.m. on August 28, Army troops and police entered the Zócalo to beat and forcibly remove the activists remaining in the plaza.

The march was a great success. Student leaders estimated the number of participants had been close to one million. Some newspapers looked favorably on the demonstration, recounting the applause and shouts of support for the students that came from passersby on the buildings and sidewalks. However, many other papers condemned the students for ringing the cathedral bells, hoisting a red and black flag over the Zócalo, and carrying posters depicting foreign revolutionaries. In turn, a

10. "Ondeó la Bandera Rojinegra en el Asta Monumental," *El Heraldo de México*, August 28, 1968.

The army clearing the Zócalo on August 28, 1968. Photo courtesy of Marcellino Perelló, personal files.

counter-movement, tied to right-of-center political and Catholic activists, argued that the students had desecrated the cathedral and the political center of power. In the days following the student protest, counter-demonstrators from across the city gathered in the Zócalo to sing the national anthem, chant patriotic slogans, and decry the protesters' actions. Despite the support offered the protesters by the bishop of Mexico City and many priests, Catholic women gathered in the Zócalo to pray and demonstrate their support for the government.

The August march and protests marked a growing schism within the Mexican populace. Despite increased violence and growing opposition from right-leaning groups, students planned for other demonstrations. The Great Silent March, as the September 13 demonstration became known, reflected what the students had learned from their earlier mistakes. Now they sought to deny the press further ammunition for questioning the movement's goals. Prior to the march, the CNH circulated statements asking activists and others not to display images of Ernesto "Che" Guevara and Ho Chi Minh. Instead, the CNH called upon students to carry images of Mexican heroes to document their commitment to the ideals of the Revolution and the Mexican constitution. Using such images challenged the idea that student activists were foreign-led and manipulated. To ensure that students did not chant anti-government slogans or any other slogans that could have been deemed offensive to the government and the press, the march was to be silent, in keeping with the tradition of nonviolent protests.

The CNH, various committees, and the brigades circulated flyers throughout the city inviting workers, parents, community leaders, intellectuals, and all the Mexican people, to join them in the march on September 13. In the meantime, letters of support for the students arrived throughout August and September. Many of these letters came from neighborhood councils in the Federal Districts, particularly from those barrios in which the occupying police and *granaderos* were harassing the residents.

Based on the nonviolent methods of protest pioneered by Mahatma Gandhi and Martin Luther King, Jr., the march of September 13, 1968, remains a pivotal event in the history of the movement. The Great Silent March began at 3:00 p.m. when students and their supporters marched from the National Museum of Anthropology and History to the Zócalo, where a mass meeting took place at 5:15. For many activists, it was the pinnacle of the movement. It represented their mass support, their seriousness, and their potential for success.

From August 27 to September 13, students demonstrated to the government that they were the vanguard of a popular movement that challenged the business-as-usual attitude of the governing groups. Published statements of support and growing numbers of demonstrators in the student-led marches reflected the broad base of support that the youth enjoyed. With the opening of the Olympics quickly approaching, President Díaz Ordaz and the members of his government desperately needed to gain control of an increasingly embarrassing situation. International news journalists started to join the sportswriters who had already arrived in Mexico to cover the Olympic time trials; these journalists began to report on the growing protests taking place in the country that was slated to host the Olympics in less than two months. In the press, on the streets, and in homes, people argued over the student movement. The student movement divided Mexican families and politicians, and caused dissent among the students themselves, just as anti-Vietnam War protests did in the United States. Although the September 13 march was a success, the level of violence had been escalating throughout August and September, and in the end the students' designs for a bright new future and public dialogue were dashed only five short days after one of their most successful demonstrations.

The government's struggle to take control of UNAM, one of the institutions that students had occupied, began on September 18, 1968, at

Students representing the sciences. Photo courtesy of Marcellino Perelló, personal files.

9:40 p.m., when fourteen large armored personnel carriers, ten small troop transports, five light tanks, and 10,000 soldiers were posted outside University City. Students in the *guardias* and those occupying the UNAM building observed the Army's movements and thought at first that the military was simply continuing its policy of intimidation. Since the students had grown accustomed to having the Army around, the initial appearance of soldiers outside the campus was not immediately alarming. Yet some students did attempt to warn others on campus attending meetings and working in the building. Twenty minutes later, one of the students' worst fears came to pass.

Shortly before 10:00 p.m., a column in full riot gear entered through the gates of UNAM. The invasion had begun. Chaos gripped the activists. Some were able to flee the area into the surrounding neighborhoods. Once inside UNAM, the military forces began to conduct a building-by-building search removing all the inhabitants they found. By 10:30 p.m., the military had occupied many of the departments and colleges as well as the esplanade. People outside UNAM began to suspect that something was wrong at Ciudad Universitaria (University City; CU) only when, at 10:25 p.m., Radio UNAM ceased operation without warning. Journalists flocked to University City to cover the story as the invasion unfolded. Though many reporters were witnesses to the operation, the subsequent newspaper reports differed in the details. Some journalists stated that a military spokesperson fed them the story they were to print. The newspaper *El Día* reported: "The soldiers showed the journalists a box of empty soda bottles stopped up with pieces of cloth that were supposed to be Molotov cocktails. The journalists did not see any other types of arms during our stay in the university."[11]

Though the invasion of UNAM targeted student activists and their supporters, it caught many bystanders and residents of University City in its snare. As the soldiers moved through the buildings, they found unlikely "activists" at the CU. In the Facultad de Economía (School of Economics) building, the Comité de lucha (Committee of the Struggle) was hosting a parents' meeting at the time of the attack, and sympathetic parents were detained along with the students. The military also detained people who were usually there at night—custodial workers, broadcast journalists for Radio UNAM, as well as students and their families who lived in the neighborhood.

By midnight, the Army demanded that all journalists and photographers leave the campus. Shortly after midnight, the Army began to place the detained into military vehicles. Some of the prisoners were taken to Lecumberri prison; others were taken to local facilities. Estimates of the numbers of detainees ranged from the government's figure of 500 to eyewitness Esteban Bravo's estimate of 800, to the North American Congress on Latin America's (NACLA) anonymous source who claimed that 3,000 were captured.[12] By 3:45 a.m., the Army was in control of University City. All journalists, students, professors, and staff had been cleared from the campus. UNAM had fallen with little resistance.

Secretary of the Interior Luis Echeverría, working with the Army, had made the tactical decision to invade UNAM. Throughout the summer of 1968, UNAM had been a center of student activity, where students enjoyed the support of the faculty, administration, and staff. On the campus, activists had access to office equipment and the kind of protected space that was a necessity for organizational purposes. Wresting the campus from the students would undermine the movement and weaken its ability to coordinate effectively. The government again justified its actions by claiming that the university was a center of subversion, not of education. From the activists' perspective, the government showed its

---

11. *El Día*, September 19, 1968.
12. "El Ejército Ocupó la Ciudad Universitaria," *El Día*, September 19, 1968; and "Eyewitness Report," September 24, 1968, *NACLA* (November 1968), 12.

willingness to use its strength and to violate its own laws by entering UNAM. In fact, the incursion violated university autonomy. UNAM was a state-supported university, but it had its own governing apparatus with a powerful rector, who held an important political position within the PRI (the Partido Revolucionario Institucional, or the Party of the Institutional Revolution), but also enjoyed great independence. Because its other warnings had gone unheeded, the Mexican government decided to issue a comprehensive threat in the form of this military action. Its narrow purpose was to deny a central space for students to organize. More importantly, the attack demonstrated the power of the Mexican government, and its ability to assert its authority, despite whatever support the students enjoyed in the Federal District. The political elite and some members of the general public had grown tired of the student movement and were prepared to end the protest without meeting student demands.

Angry reactions to the invasion erupted the following day. Playing the role of a distant father, Díaz Ordaz was absent from much of the public discussion regarding the invasion. Instead, the offices of Luis Echeverría responded, as did the Secretary of Defense, Marcelino García Barragán. Echeverría issued a statement claiming that the government was justified in the invasion because the buildings occupied by students in the university were the "property of the nation and destined to be used for public service."[13] Echeverría argued that the buildings on the UNAM campus had been occupied and used illegally since the end of July, and that the buildings were not being used for their main purpose, academic study. He insisted that the students had exercised their right to make public demands, but they had done so in a manner that was "antisocial and possibly dangerous." The office of the Secretary of the Interior also stated that the government was within its constitutional rights to forcefully remove individuals who did not have any right to be on the campus because they were not students.

The retaking of UNAM drew criticism of, but also support for, the administration. Condemnation came from both the political left and right and from within and beyond the university, but many people also supported the government's actions, arguing that the purpose of the university was to educate not serve as a site for political protests. Supporters of the students were particularly vehement in their outrage. Newspaper editorials protested the use of force against the students and the

---

13. "El Ejército Ocupó la Ciudad Universitaria," *El Día*, September 19, 1968.

university.[14] The university rector Barros Sierra condemned the acts of the Mexican government, while unions, students, and professors echoed his sentiment.

On September 25, amid growing strikes in the provinces, Mexico City newspapers proclaimed the news that UNAM Rector Barros Sierra had resigned. His letter of resignation reiterated his plea that violence against the students must cease. He wrote: "The problems of the youth may only be resolved by the route of education, never by force, violence, or corruption. This has been my constant rule of action and the object of my complete dedication, in time and energy, during my time as rector."[15] A member of the PRI and appointed by the president, Barros Sierra went on to state that he had been a victim of personal attacks and defamation. He condemned the invasion and the continued occupations of campuses, and he again criticized those who did not attempt to understand the students or his pleas for peaceful solutions.

Violence continued throughout the city. Street battles between *granaderos* and students escalated when the Army moved in to occupy IPN. Students affiliated with Poli fought *granaderos* in the Nonoalco-Tlatelolco housing complex where, it was reported, the students confronted tear gas and armed with Molotov cocktails they flung at the troops and used to burn two "official vehicles." The students and *granaderos* struggled for hours. The students intercepted fifteen to sixteen buses that were passing through the area. They used the buses to create barricades blocking the roads leading into the housing complex. In those areas that were not blockaded, students punctured the tires of official cars. The battle between students and *granaderos* resulted in the death of a *granadero* and the injury of three police officers. Bystanders and residents of the housing complex were injured, as were students. According to a newspaper account, nineteen students, two of whom were women, were detained.[16]

Once in control, the Army then decided to blockade and occupy Tlatelolco itself, using nine tanks and 500 troops to restore order. The Saturday and Sunday confrontations between students and *granaderos* in the Nonoalco-Tlatelolco housing area were the most violent confrontations

14. See, for example, Gilberto Keith, "Un hecho Triste: La Fuerza Otra Vez," *Excélsior*, September 19, 1968.
15. Letter to Junta de Gobierno de la Universidad Nacional Autónoma de México from University Rector Javier Barros Sierra; text reprinted in *El Heraldo*, September 23, 1968.
16. "Por 6 horas grupos de jóvenes hacen frente a la fuerza pública; un granderos muerto" *Novedades*, September 22, 1968.

of 1968 between students and government forces. Violence continued throughout the Federal District. Students burned buses and other vehicles, and riots and street battles erupted at UNAM, Poli, and around the National Museum of Anthropology.

Following the riots, newspapers reported that the cost of the damage to the Nonoalco-Tlatelolco areas was estimated to be in the millions of pesos.[17] United States Defense Intelligence Reports estimated a loss of thirty million pesos (approximately 4.2 million dollars) in Mexico City business. Along with those losses, 803 buses, 10 street cars, 4 ambulances, 16 police motorcycles, and 6 radio control police cars had been destroyed or vandalized. Other damage included vandalism to street lights and signs. Mexican journalists began to draw similarities between these student protests and those in France and the United States.

Faced with the violence and chaos in the city, various professors and school directors sought to achieve some coherence in leadership. A group of professors and directors, supported by teachers and employees of UNAM, sent a letter asking the Governing Junta of UNAM to reject Barros Sierra's resignation in the hope that he could negotiate some sort of truce with Secretary of the Interior Echeverría. The governing board of UNAM then declined to accept Barros Sierra's resignation, and he rescinded his resignation and continued as rector throughout the crisis. As university faculty and administrators hoped he would, Barros Sierra demanded that the Army leave the UNAM campus. On September 30, 1968, 1,300 soldiers withdrew from UNAM with the government's request that the university return to its focus on education. The strike continued despite the request to return to the work of education by resuming classes.

On October 1, once UNAM was back in the hands of university personnel, the CNH held a press conference on October 1 to discuss the continuation of the protest and strike; meanwhile, representatives from the CNH were publicly negotiating their demands with the government. El Día reported that, during the press conference, a North American journalist asked if the students had enough power to force the government into a dialogue, or if they believed further violence would be necessary. The students simply responded by saying that they had the right to ask the government to listen to them.[18] Another journalist inquired if the students would hold demonstrations during the Olympics. The students

---

17. "Cuantiosos Daños en Tlatelolco," El Heraldo, September 23, 1968.
18. "La situación estudiantil," El Día, October 1, 1968.

were reported as having said, "If it is necessary to have a demonstration during it [the Olympic Games], then we will."[19]

Massacre and Cleansing of Records: The Impact of 1968

At the end of the conference, the CNH called for a 5:00 p.m. meeting for the next day in the Plaza of Three Cultures in Tlatelolco. But people were already gathering in the plaza by 4:00. Because the meeting was being held in such a large complex, there were bystanders and apartment dwellers there as well. The CNH arrived and installed itself on the third floor of the Chihuahua apartment building, close to the cathedral and overlooking the plaza. From that position, the council leaders could address the crowd. The meeting, which was not as large as previous ones (only an estimated 10,000 to 20,000 people attended), began in fairly predictable fashion, with speakers addressing the issues of the movement. The Army was present on the side streets, but the presence of tanks had become a common sight at the demonstrations across the city. Because the meeting was smaller, and because the military was blockading their path around the plaza, the student leaders decided to suspend the planned march. Details are murky regarding what occurred after 5:30 p.m. because of conflicting stories from the press and from eyewitnesses. But it appears that at approximately 6:00, helicopters flying over the plaza illuminated it with high-powered search-lights. Shots then rang out from the rooftops and around the plaza. The massacre had begun.

For the next four hours, students, military, police, and undercover agents fought in the Plaza of Three Cultures. Many civilians and bystanders—in addition to activists, protesters, students, their parents, and journalists—were injured and killed. The massacre of October 2 remains shrouded in mystery. How many people lost their lives in the plaza: 49, 200, 300, 700, or more? Initial reports suggested that 29 died, 80 were injured, and 1,000 were detained. Ultimately, the official number of dead was set at 49. International journalists who were in the plaza and who subsequently visited the hospitals and morgues reported that more than 300 died in the plaza.

Both sides of the political spectrum expressed shock and outrage at the massacre. The Minister of Defense argued that students fired

---

19. "Salen las tropes de la universidad," *Novedades*, October 1, 1968.

on the soldiers and police first; the students argued the opposite. The government took action to maintain national unity and support. In the Chamber of Deputies, representatives debated a statement of support for the government that had to respond to an influence of foreign and revolutionary agitators who had gained control of the Mexican youth. The statement triggered fierce discussion, and fighting broke out in the Chamber. The right-of-center PAN leader Diego Fernandez de Ceballaos came to blows with the mayor of Mexico City and PRI member Ricardo Reglado regarding a show of support for the government. Within both the PAN and PRI, members of the two parties disagreed with each other over a show of support for the executive branch. In turn, senators and representatives from the two parties issued statements of both support and criticism. Prominent Mexican revolutionary figures such as former-General and former-President Lázaro Cárdenas publicly criticized the Díaz Ordaz administration and asked for a peaceful solution. This was an unprecedented act; no previous president had ever criticized another, and an outcry followed. A day later, Cárdenas issued a follow-up statement in which he appealed for national unity and criticized supposed foreign provocateurs who sought to undermine Mexico.

Though a number of countries, including the United States, debated their participation in the Olympics, none withdrew, and the 1968 Olympics opened on October 14 to great fanfare. While the 1968 Olympics showcased much of Mexican culture, it also was a venue for multiple protests, as seen in the famous photo by John Dominis of the 200-meter dash athletes Tommie Smith and John Carlos raising black-gloved fists while the U.S. national anthem played. In his autobiography, Smith argued that the gesture was to recognize the human rights of Black athletes.[20] A recognition of political and social change also took place when the delegation from Cuba received a standing ovation, and Díaz Ordaz received cursory respectful applause.

The movement limped along in the months following October 2. Many activists had been arrested during the summer. Those not arrested during the protests found themselves hunted by the authorities. Some activists fled into exile, while the police arrested others. Leaders of the students, parents, and professors were put on trial and received sentences of up to sixteen years of hard labor. For the first anniversary of what

---

20. Tommie Smith and David Steele, *Silent Gesture: The Autobiography of Tommie Smith* (Philadelphia: Temple University Press, 2008), 38–40.

became known as the Tlatelolco massacre, a few families of activists who were imprisoned and fellow students gathered in the Plaza of Three Cultures. For years to come, the campuses of UNAM and Poli experienced a greater police presence around the times of the anniversaries. Resistance, however, came in other forms, such as through literature, music, art, and fashion. Mexican youth embraced the counterculture post-1968.

In the following years, activists regained their voices and publicly commemorated the 1968 massacre with marches, conferences, and even reenactments on the anniversary of the massacre. Many of those imprisoned in the later 1960s were granted amnesty beginning in the 1970s. Some of those who led the movement found jobs in the government of Luis Echeverría and in the universities. In the mid-1970s, ex-activists began to write about their experiences in the movement.[21] They founded oppositional newspapers and political magazines and organized the Mexican feminist and gay rights movement. Some left university studies and joined revolutionary movements or began organizing workers. Others continued to demand answers to what happened in the summer of 1968. Ex-members of the CNH and other activists became leaders in the contemporary Mexican human rights movement. They have linked with other Mexican social movements to demand that the government—which not only failed to respond to the events of 1968 but also subsequently committed many other violent acts—be held accountable for its actions. Activists demanded access to their security files and to all government documentation regarding social movements. When elected in 2000, Vicente Fox—an ex-Coca Cola executive, member of PAN (National Action Party), and the first president elected from an opposition party since 1910—responded to the demands and opened the files.

On October 2, 1968, the government chose violence over a peaceful resolution, but the students were never completely quieted. Instead, their voices and actions represented the growing dissent that encircled the PRI party and its authoritarian one-party rule. The student propaganda machine chugged along, even during the years immediately following the crisis of power that began in the summer of 1968. When Luis Echeverría became president in 1970, he seemed attentive to some of the

21. The most widely studied compilation of testimonials is Elena Poniatowska, *Massacre in Mexico* (Columbia: University of Missouri Press, 1991). Activists' writings include Luis González de Alba, *Los días y los años* (México: Era, 1971), and more recently Roberta Avedaño Martínez, *De la libertad y el encierro* (México: La idea dorada, 1998).

1968 activists marching on October 2, 2008, the fortieth anniversary of the Tlatelolco massacre. The banner displays reproductions of student propaganda from 1968. Photo courtesy of Elaine Carey, personal files.

students' demands and initiated a number of the democratic reforms. Many student protesters were granted amnesty; others received scholarships to study for advanced degrees within Mexico and abroad, and other ex-activists received university appointments. The historical record and evidence, however, remained equally obscure in the 1970s and 1980s.[22] Despite the cleansing of the blood from Tlatelolco and the official scrubbing of the historical record, the generation of 1968 continued a search for answers. As with the student movement, the Mexican Dirty War, which the PRI-dominated government conducted in the 1960s and 70s against student and guerilla groups (and of which the Tlatelolco Massacre was one of many "dirty" incidents), remained on the periphery of historical consciousness. The inability of the government to stem the flow of dissent, and its violent response to the student protests, only further tarnished its image. The events of 1968, combined with the

---

22. New research challenges that putative obscurity: see Louise Walker, *Waking from the Dream: Mexico's Middle Classes after 1968* (Stanford University Press, 2013), and Alex Aviña, *Specters of Revolution: Peasant Guerrilla in the Cold War Mexican Countryside* (New York: Oxford University Press, 2014).

Secondary school students marching on October 2, 2008, the fortieth anniversary of the Tlatelolco massacre. The sign says "More funding for education; October 2, never forget!" Photo courtesy of Elaine Carey, personal files.

continuing economic crisis that emerged in the late 1980s, contributed to the decline of the party.

The demands of the students and their supporters that emerged in 1968 would continue to grow. As noted, in 2000, the right-of-center president from the National Action Party (PAN), Vicente Fox, oversaw the opening of the archives that documented crimes against young people, workers, social activists, artists, and journalists who engaged in social activism. In 2001, he appointed Dr. Ignacio Carrillo Prieto as Mexico's Special Prosecutor for Social and Political Movements, and Prieto pursued cases against certain public officials who had been accused of human rights violations during the 1960s and 70s. Many activists demanded that the surviving leaders of the 1968 government be put on trial, and this led to the house arrest of several key political figures such as Echeverría. Instead of standing trial for murder, however, these officials were found guilty of the lesser charge of kidnapping, and most were released by 2006. Though the surviving activists differ on whether key political figures should be tried for genocide, imprisoned, or forgiven, they all look upon 1968 as a pivotal time in Mexican history. In 2006 the government finally, and officially, confirmed that 12 massacres, 120 extrajudicial killings,

800 forced disappearances, and 2,000 acts of torture against detainees occurred in that turbulent year. Despite the good work done by the office of the Special Prosecutor in documenting these crimes and producing the report—with the help of scholars, activists, and bureaucrats—the office of the Special Prosecutor was dismantled shortly after the end of Fox's term as president in 2006. Despite the closing of the office, activism surrounding the movement continues. Former activists have captured the movement and its impact in modern Mexican literature and film. As noted, every year, mass marches take place on October 2 commemorating the massacre but also demanding an end to impunity and a demand for human rights: "October 2, no se olvide" (Never forget October 2).

Sources

Two Student-Produced Posters

During the movement, students did not have access to the mainstream press, so they used posters and banners to convey their messages. In Mexico and throughout Latin America, walls are painted with political slogans to support candidates for elections, but public spaces are also used for anti-government propaganda. It is a popular form of expression. Students embraced this form to motivate solidarity among workers, professors, teachers, parents, intellectuals, and artists. With their occupations of schools and universities, they gained access to materials needed to produce posters, banners, and flyers that the brigades distributed. Here are two such forms of student-produced propaganda.

The Gorilla behind the Mask

In the first poster, the slogan reads: "The police and military kill your best children." The small print reads: "The students and people unmask those in the service of the CIA." Two arrows, pointing toward the mask and the gorilla's body are tagged "GOBIERNO" (GOVERNMENT). A piece of newspaper emerging from the gorilla's ear reads "Abusive Press."

Colección de impresos Esther Montero, Archivo Histórico de Universidad Nacional Autónoma de México Centro de Estudios sobre la Universidad Biblioteca Nacional, México, D.F. By permission.

The emblem of the Olympics may be seen in the corner with the images of a gorilla in each ring. In the right corner, a small CNH identifies that leadership that produced the image.

Questions for Consideration

What is the full message of this poster? Why would the students employ such images? Why did they target the press as also abusive?

❖❖❖❖❖

All of Echeverría's Men

This second student-produced image depicts national and local leaders: Luis Cueto Ramírez (Director of Police), Rodolfo Mendiolea Cerecero (Sub-director of Police), Armando Frías (Commander of the Granaderos), Alfonso Corona del Rosal (Regent of Mexico City), and

From the collection of the University Museum of Contemporary Art (MUAC). The National Autonomous University of Mexico. By Permission.

Luis Echeverría (Secretary of the Interior). They hover over a *calavera soldadera* (skeleton of a female soldier).

Questions for Consideration

How are the politicians presented? What is the role of the *calavera*? Why is she lying on the Mexican Constitution? Why is Luis Echeverría holding and pulling her boot? What is the full message of this poster?

◆◆◆◆◆

The Voice of Mexico, 1968[23]

On December 1, 2008, *All Things Considered*, a broadcast of National Public Radio, aired "Mexico 1968: A Movement, a Massacre, and a

23. "Mexico 68: A Movement, A Massacre, and the 40-year Search for Truth," Radio Diaries, http://www.radiodiaries.org/mexico-68-a-movement-a-massacre-and-the-40-year-search-for-the-truth/ (accessed April 18, 2016).

Forty-Year Search for Truth," produced by Anayansi Díaz and Joe Richman. For the interviews, Díaz sought activists who wished to talk to her but who also spoke English. In 1968, many university students in Mexico did not study English but rather French or Russian. Complicating the process was the reality that due to the violence that took place in 1968 and long thereafter, many activists feared reprisals if they spoke to a journalist. With the opening of the archives, beginning in 2000, more people were willing to talk.

Questions for Consideration

In your reading of the interviews, what do the activists tell you about Mexico in 1968? How do they portray the movement? What was significant about the movement in the eyes of the activists? How far do you think a historian can trust forty-year-old memories that are articulated in a public medium? In other words, what is the potential value and usefulness of these oral histories, and what are their potential pitfalls and drawbacks? Regardless of potential problems with these testimonies, what insights do you take away from them?

◆ ◆ ◆ ◆ ◆

MARCELA FERNANDEZ DE VIOLANTE, STUDENT: We were very young, very naive. But for the first time, you had this notion that this country was going to be changed by the power of our convictions.

MIGUEL BRESEDA, STUDENT: You would get in a bus and give a speech and inform the people. Because newspapers wouldn't publish anything. And people would give you money, they would congratulate you and they would say, "We are with you young people . . ."

DAVID HUERTA, STUDENT: There was this sense of excitement and adventure. And the problem was growing, steadily day after day. It sort of entered into the fabric of Mexico City. What we were seeing was a waking society.

MARTA ACEVEDO, STUDENT: Then, the 27th of August came. And I think it was the highest moment of the movement.

(CHANTING: ¡VIVA EL MOVIMIENTO ESTUANDITIL!)

SERGIO AGUAYO, HISTORIAN: Never before in the history of Mexico, half a million people went out to the street to protest, to challenge the authority of the President. And numbers in history and politics matter. I mean, if ten people protest, well that's dissent. When half a million people protest, then that's the beginning of social revolution.

MARCELINO PERELLO, STUDENT LEADER: We were asking for the President to go out and to speak to us....

MIGUEL BRESEDA: The Zócalo, the main square, was lit with burning tires. There was dancing, guitars. A little bottle of tequila there and over there.

MARCELINO PERELLO: It was unforgettable. We were dreamers. And we were very happy.

MIGUEL BRESEDA: So we are there. And the doors of the Palace open and the soldiers come out and they stand in front of us. And say, "Señores se les ha permitido hacer su manifestación y se les solicita que abandonen la plaza. Gentlemen, You have been allowed to make your demonstration, and now you have to leave the plaza." And I remember the whistles and yelling and all of that. And, "We are not leaving!" Holding arms all of us. And saying, "We're not moving." And they take out their bayonets, and put them in their rifles and they start walking towards us.

MARIO NUÑEZ MARIEL, STUDENT: And you can hear when the army walks with the bayonets; it's a noise you will never forget.

DAVID HUERTA: I remember that some of the students decided that we had weapons in our pockets. Big twenty-cent coins that were made of copper. Very huge coins, and heavy.

Some of the students threw those coins against the soldiers. And you know what happened? The soldiers stopped to pick up those coins. It was not really that much money, twenty cents. But for them, it was. I mean, the soldiers, our enemies, were the same age as us. If you take the uniform out of a soldier, what you discover behind is a poor, young peasant. In a way, weren't we fighting for them? Sort of an eye-opener.

✦✦✦✦✦

"Bloody Tlatelolco": An Editorial Published in *Excélsior*, October 3, 1968[24]

On October 2, 1968, the festive atmosphere that had taken place at many student-led meetings disappeared. On that day, the Army and police opened fire on the students and bystanders gathered in the plaza. The massacre that took place rocked the city. Newspaper editors had to report the events that took place, but they had to do so very carefully since they received government funding.

Questions for Consideration

In reading this document, consider the tone and use of language. How does the editor juxtapose youth versus adults? What tone and message is the editor hoping to convey? Does he or she side with either the students or the government? How should the historian use this as a source? In other words, what are its values and what are its limitations?

✦✦✦✦✦

24. "Mexico 68: A Movement, a Massacre, and the 40-year Search for Truth," Radio Diaries, http://www.radiodiaries.org/mexico-68-a-movement-a-massacre-and-the-40-year-search-for-the-truth/ (accessed April 18, 2016).

A plague has invaded the Mexican capital, the heart of the Republic. The army claimed that it had to disperse a meeting that was held in the Plaza of Three Cultures, but their presence left an appalling amount of blood and bodies. Within the consciousness of sensitive citizens infinite despair and distress have developed.

The reason is because last night the Army's actions gave no clear answers. By contrast, they have created new grievances. The intransigence and force of the government only serve to widen the gap of resentment warding off any possibility for reconciliation.

While it is true that students—and a number of teachers— have exhibited behavior that at times exceeded reasonableness, coming from insolence and overestimating their strength in the challenge.

The arrogance of the students who demanded that the President of the Republic appear in the Zócalo to talk to protesters on the same day he had to submit his report to the nation was childish and arrogant.

The bloodshed demands a dramatic and thorough review of action to determine responsibility. It is not by killing each other that we will build the Mexico we, despite our differences, love and cherish.

Nevertheless, the government is comprised of adults, people who should know about blinding pride. How often is love resented? Adults know that juvenile ardor and passion lead to futile and dangerous insolence. However, adulthood must work for a future, and we expect its grandeur.

Epilogue: The Streets Speak, 1968 and Today

Elaine Carey

"The beautiful youth showed up to change it from winter to spring."[1]

In 2011, mass uprisings spread across North Africa and the Middle East, igniting the "Arab Spring." Citizens from all levels of society—activists, professionals, workers, parents, children, and soldiers—all hoped to end the long winters of authoritarianism. In North Africa, these revolts ousted political leaders Zine al-Abidine Ben Ali in Tunisia, Hosni Mubarak in Egypt, and Muammar Gadhafi in Libya. The violence that erupted in Libya triggered factional fighting and led to the death of Gadhafi. Popular uprisings continued in other parts of the Middle East, including Syria and Yemen, and these protests escalated in the wake of Gadhafi's death.

Before 2011, political scientists and analysts had long argued that the authoritarianism, dictatorships, and corruption found in the governments of the Middle East might eventually result in mass popular uprisings. There were all kinds of warning signs. Record numbers of college-educated young people (who were better-educated than their parents or grandparents) graduated only to discover that few economic opportunities existed for them. The nationalist regimes that emerged from the old colonial empires failed to implement promised economic, social, and political reforms. Autocracy, corruption, inflation, lack of personal and political freedoms, brutality, and unemployment—problems that remain across much of the region—were rife in the houses of Ben Ali, Mubarak, and Gadhafi and ultimately led to their downfall.

In 2011, the same year of the Arab Spring, protests erupted across the United States. Activists, both young and old, erected tents and occupied major city centers—most notably the Wall Street District in New York City, home to the U.S. Stock Exchange—to protest the lack of economic opportunity and the growing economic inequality between the top

---

1. From "Sout al-Horeya" (The Voice of Freedom) by Amir Eid and Hany Adel: https://www.youtube.com/watch?v=PAEt6QJJi-c (accessed August 15, 2015). I would like to thank my colleague Nerina Rustimji for her assistance on this epilogue.

1 percent of the population and the majority 99 percent. The collapse of the United States' housing market in 2008 rippled across the world, leading to bailouts of major banks while unemployment rates and housing foreclosures continued to rise.[2] Although the controversial measures in banking during the housing crisis undertaken by the administration of President Barack Obama were instrumental in averting an economic meltdown in the United States and, consequently, across the globe, many of the factors that precipitated the crisis went unresolved, especially the growing disparity between "haves" and "have nots." It is no coincidence that the presidential race of 2016 has seen, in the spring of 2016, strong and enthusiastic support for populist insurgents on both the Left and the Right who propose radically different solutions to these inequities.

The Occupy Wall Street (OWS) movement drew its inspiration from the events that unfolded during the Arab Spring. As in Tunisia, Egypt, and Libya, activists organized through social networking. In turn, OWS protests spread in Europe, and violent confrontations unfolded in Greece, Spain, and Italy. Greeks, Spaniards, and Italians of all ages rioted over the economic austerity programs negotiated by their governments in order to receive bailouts from the International Monetary Fund, the World Bank, and the European Union. It was only in the late summer of 2015 that Greece appeared to be on the road to fiscal stability after four contentious years that witnessed continuous, widespread protests.

The case studies in this book seem distant to the unfolding dramas that rocked much of the world in 2011 and continue to reverberate down to today. But are they? It is true that in 1968, the United States, Mexico, and France were not in the midst of a global economic collapse. On the contrary: each of these countries was still enjoying the post-World War II economic and population boom that contributed to a dramatic increase in the number of college-educated citizens. Regardless of this difference, there are some striking parallels between the protest movements of today and those of 1968. In 1968, activists of all ages questioned bureaucratic Soviet-style Communism, capitalism, authoritarianism, imperialism, and democracy. Equally, since 2011 protests around the globe have been driven by a multiplicity of frustrations, discontentments, and causes for violent anger over the economic collapse of 2008, austerity measures in much

---

2. From 2008 through 2011, 414 smaller banks collapsed in the United States and went into receivership, with most of these failed banks acquired by larger entities. In the five years before 2008, a total of 11 banks had failed.

of Europe, and growing concerns about overall socio-economic decline. In 1968, as today, people across the globe expressed their solidarity with protests in other parts of the world. In many ways, the movements of the past connected to each other in ways that echo into the present. As Mauricio Borrero discusses in his treatment of Eastern Europe in 1968 in Chapter 3, the current uprisings have created a general climate of activism that is unique in each case to local circumstances but global in its connections. As in 1968, the global protests of 2011–2012 and following have had an ability to communicate their messages across space and through time, but today that ability is of much greater speed and reach. Today's protests, as was true in 1968, also exhibit diverse actors in varied roles and equally have aroused the suspicion of leadership and leaders.

Media Use

In 1968, activists found that the mainstream press sensationalized their exploits or ignored their demands and focused instead on governmental responses. As a result, students and their supporters created their own means to communicate; they overcame the obstacle of censorship via new creative outlets. In Mexico, China, France, and Eastern Europe, students circulated their messages and demands through the use of posters, banners, graffiti, and student presses. As photographer and historian Patrice Olsen has argued, the use of stencils, banners, flyers, and posters during demonstrations and social movements ensured that—despite censorship—the streets spoke for the activists.[3] In turn, television and newspaper journalists photographed and filmed the protests and the protesters' messages, preserving for posterity the narrative created by the students as an alternative to that circulated in government-dominated newspapers, radio, and television. Through these slogans, banners, graffiti, and alternative news sources, the protesters endeavored to persuade other sectors of society to join the cause.

Journalists also interviewed activists, seeking out vocal demonstrators and leaders. This too has happened more recently when journalists filmed the posters of activists from New York City to Yemen, thereby giving these protestors a global platform on which to voice their demands and inspire

---

3. Patrice Olsen, Mexican Studies Meeting, Congress on Latin American History, Chicago, IL, January 7, 2012.

solidarity. In the opening days of the revolution in Syria (before the revolution degenerated into civil war), secondary school students voiced their and the masses' discontent with President Bashar Assad, whose family has governed the country since 1970, in graffiti on school walls. In brief, graffiti, banners, posters, and flyers have continuously served to motivate people—even those who have endured hardships due to violence—to continue to protest.

Unlike in 1968, activists today have greater control over how their messages circulate, and they easily bypass attempts to censor or control access to media. In Tunisia, street vendor Mohamed Bouazizi's self-immolation after months of harassment by municipal authorities led to outrage, and people used electronic social networking to express their rage at a government that appeared to hinder its citizens' ability to survive and earn a living. Despite the controversy of whether people expressing solidarity with the fruit vendor Bouazizi (or with a college student with the same name) used social networking to organize a protest, it remains clear that the use of technology ensured that news of the protests spread unfettered by government censors. Young Egyptians, motivated to protest by the events in Tunisia, first tested the waters of opposition by chanting slogans about food and rent costs in different Cairo neighborhoods. These vocal slogans later became visual, in the form of banners and posters but also as YouTube and Facebook postings, becoming permanent and far-ranging indictments against the Mubarak regime.

Globalization in the latter decades of the twentieth century triggered the laying of fiber optic lines and the launching of satellites to facilitate communication. While cellular and smartphones can be employed as instruments of governmental control, these tools also can be harnessed to circumvent those same methods of control. Today, activists communicate instantaneously with people across the globe via social networking sites such as Facebook, Tumblr, Instagram, Flickr, and Twitter. No longer do activists wait for journalists to deem their posters, banners, or speeches as worthy of screen time or print space. Moreover, they share ideas face-to-face via Skype and other personal communication tools. In 1968, such exchanges of ideas took place in person via jet-air travel that allowed activists from distant lands to meet more quickly than ever before. What seemed fast and technologically advanced in 1968 now appears slow and insignificant when compared with today's instant digital global messaging. As the strongmen encountered opposition during the Arab Spring, they attempted to control the flow of information with blackouts and continued surveillance. Peaceful social-movement activists used social media to spread information regarding protest marchers; they were later joined by such terror groups as the Islamic State of Iraq and al-Sham (better known as *ISIS* or *ISIL*), which also post their messages on YouTube and other platforms, thereby providing instantaneous messages and coverage of their actions. The Islamic State has also discovered that these electronic media are effective tools for recruiting disaffected youth from around the world. In response, governments opposed to the Islamic State have begun to use the same media as a means of broadcasting counter messages.

Expressions of Discontent

Music too held sway in 1968 as a means to communicate ideas, discontentment, and demands. Certain American musicians, such as Joan Baez and Bob Dylan, had a global audience in 1968 when musicians around the globe translated their lyrics and sang their songs, several of which became iconic anthems. A new genre, *La nueva canción*, emerged in the 1960s when Latin American musicians adapted traditional folk music to suit a more contemporary, and global, audience. They also embraced rock music; musicians translated the lyrics of popular English rock tunes as well as wrote and performed their own songs. Universities, colleges, and their surrounding neighborhoods became focal points for this new music scene. The Mexican, French, and Eastern European protest music that emerged in the 1960s was catchy, with lyrics that were easy to remember, such as "Il est cinq heures Paris S'eveille" ("It's 5 a.m. and Paris Wakes Up"), and simple melodies. Similarly catchy chants and protest music have today found new audiences as activists sing about their solidarity. Protest songs from the past—including "L'Internationale," the Communist Anthem, which students sang around the world in 1968—have enjoyed a rebirth. And, of course, new songs have arisen as sources of inspiration and communication across borders, just as they did in the 1960s. "The Voice of Freedom" by Amir Eid and Hany Adel, which went viral on YouTube and various social networks, has been translated from Arabic into many different languages, and has thus become an anthem with a global audience. The U.S.-based group Emma's Revolution celebrated the Arab Spring in its song "Rise" before penning and recording "Occupy the USA," one of the anthems of the Occupy Wall Street movement. Musicians and demonstrators continue to protest the wars in Iraq and Afghanistan as well as the Israeli occupation of Palestinian lands. Likewise, in Vladimir Putin's Russia, the feminist punk-rock group Pussy Riot has been a voice of protest.

As in 1968, participants in the protest movements of today, whether on the Left or the Right, are generally suspicious of those in power and of any centralized leadership. Yet there are, and have always been, exceptions. As we read in Zachary Scarlett's treatment on China in Chapter 1, Mao Zedong co-opted willing and often blindly loyal students and other young people as he attempted to harness their political power. And as Borrero documents in Chapter 3, Eastern European activists were motivated by their own governmental leaders to challenge Soviet authority. In Poland, Czechoslovakia, and Yugoslavia, these moments of self-determination contributed to mass uprisings supported by national political leaders. The Soviet Union could not erase the national histories of those countries that, for many decades prior to World War II, considered themselves as part of the capitalist Western world. In turn, these uprisings threatened the power of the Soviet Union.

Despite the Soviet Union's ability to squash the protests in 1968, fissures had been created that slowly destroyed the Soviet Union. Playwrights, writers, and artists within the Soviet bloc continued to voice their dissent regardless of the threats and prison sentences. Their plays and music found a growing audience in underground bars and theaters. Supporters smuggled out and translated their works for a growing foreign audience who wanted to know what life was like behind the Iron Curtain. At the end of the 1980s, due to costly military expenditures, a disastrous Soviet intervention in Afghanistan, political calcification, misguided economic policies, and nationalist and ethnic divisions, the Warsaw Pact crumbled. In December 1991, the Soviet Union's painful death throes ended with its dissolution into fifteen independent nations, and ex-activists of 1968, such as Václav Havel and the novelist Milan Kundera, were able to write about its demise.

For years prior to 1968, the Mexican government routinely courted student leaders and drafted them into the party structure. But, as I argue in Chapter 4, the activists of 1968 formed such a large leadership body that the government found it difficult to co-opt it, despite numerous attempts. In turn, these activists charted a path radically different from that of previous student movements in which the leadership was readily identified. The new alliances the students formed across the city and in the provinces further undermined the ability of the government to bring them into its structures. The multiplicity of activist leaders made it difficult for the government to identify whom to co-opt and how to harness their energies. The inability of the government to control the movement led to the massacre that took place on October 2, 1968—an event condemned for decades to come by the opposition parties as well as within the ruling party itself.

The power of Mexico's ruling party, the PRI (Partido Revolucionario Institucional, or Party of the Institutional Revolution), had been diminished in the same way that the Communist government's grip on the Soviet Union was weakened. Alternative newspapers, music, magazines, and novels focused on the PRI's corruption, nepotism, and violence. The PRI's inability to confront the economic crisis of the 1980s and 1990s resulted in its loss of control of the federal congress in 1997, of key governorships, and finally of the presidency in 2000. The Mexican activists of 1968 are still mobilizing against a government that continues to operate with impunity—in the "war against drugs," for example. Even though the PRI returned to power, civil society continues to question the ability of the Mexican government to respond correctly to violence and to respect human rights.

The events in the Middle East of 2011–2012 seem, in retrospect, to have resulted in ruling bodies that look remarkably similar to the authoritarian governments of the 1960s. The inability of the ruling class to understand the people's demands and hatred of the regime contributed to the heightened violence that ultimately led to Gadhafi's capture and execution in October 2011, a killing broadcast around the world on YouTube. Likewise, a deafness to discontent ultimately led to Hosni Mubarak's forced resignation in February 2011 and his subsequent conviction on corruption charges. In Syria, unrest with the rule of Bashar al-Assad led to protests in the spring of 2011 that were met with deadly force by the Syrian army. Military violence engendered resistance, and civil war ensued.

Diverse Voices

In Chapter 2, Félix Germain documents the marginalization that Black citizens, whether French or American, endured within the student movements. Their movements and protests often became co-opted by White activists; White activists assumed positions of leadership, pushing the Black protesters to the margins of the movement. In France and Senegal, however, Black activists organized to challenge the French government and the French colonial empire that treated them like second-class citizens even within their own nations and the West Indies. These Black activists broke with White activists to pursue the kinds of dramatic societal changes that would profoundly impact the lives of young people. By challenging the curriculum and calling into question traditional canons of literature, established approaches to history and other disciplines, these Black activists had the single greatest and most lasting effect on university-level education around the world. As a result of their efforts, U.S. colleges and universities now offer over 300 programs and degrees, BA to PhD, in African-American and Africana Studies. In France, African and Latin American studies programs also found a growing audience.

The issue of the marginality of diverse voices marks the Occupy Wall Street movement that began in September 2011. That marginality also led Latinos and African Americans—who felt the effects of the economic downturn far more keenly than did college-educated upper- and middle-class Whites—to question their roles within the movement. Moreover, the increasing volume of right-wing rhetoric that casts Mexicans and other Latin Americans as outside invaders who steal jobs, milk the economic system, and contribute to the escalation of crime (despite an actual decline in crime rates) remains a source of great distress for Latinos and other immigrants in the United States and Europe. Likewise, racial inequality and violence continue to haunt the United States.

There are, however, signs of hope. The death, while in police custody, of Freddie Gray, a twenty-five-year-old African American, on April 19, 2015, sparked riots in Baltimore, Maryland. The murders by an avowed racist of nine people in the historic Emanuel African Methodist Episcopal Church in Charleston, South Carolina did not incite rioting because of the church community's plea for peace and forgiveness. Although the deaths demonstrate the historic continuity of racial violence, their aftermaths also provide reason for a measure of optimism. Freddie Gray's death led to the indictment of six police officers, and the massacre in Charleston was the catalyst for the removal of the Confederate battle flag from the grounds of the South Carolina state capitol and movements to remove other symbols of the Confederacy elsewhere in the South.

Change usually occasions reaction. In the United States, members of the Tea Party and right-of-center political candidates, confronted by demographic and social changes, continue to cling to a mythic image of the United States that never existed. This too is reminiscent of the 1960s, when right-leaning groups organized to counter what they viewed as a shift away from the national social, economic, and cultural mores of the United States, Great Britain, France, and Germany. In 2015, these attempts to bring about a return to the past are questionable. Return to a time before the Civil Rights, women's, and gay rights movements? Return to colonialism? Take back America from an African-American president? It was during the 1960s that a rebirth of the Right took place in the United States and Europe. Initially, right-of-center politicians focused their attention on questioning the role of government and government expenditures and often could be counted on to support progressive social legislation. For example, more than 80 percent of the Republican members of Congress supported the 1965 Civil Rights Act. As immigration to the United States has increased, however, the Right has embraced heightened anti-immigrant rhetoric and has questioned the true impact of the Civil Rights and women's rights movements.

Women have become increasingly involved in the political activism of the last decade. As they did in the 1968 protests in Paris, Mexico, and Eastern Europe, young women and families have taken active roles in the recent Middle Eastern movements. Parents in these Middle Eastern nations brought their children to the protests to experience a historical moment. Young Muslim women, covered or not, have readily organized and participated in the protests. These educated young women in the streets seemed to be creating new political voices within their cultures and nations. However, recent public attacks on women in Tunisia, Egypt, and Syria seem to have had a chilling effect on their participation in protests. The rise of political, fundamentalist Islam has also undermined women's activism and the political gains that women made during the Arab Spring.

The women of 1968 also found a collective political voice. Building on their participation in the movements of the 1960s, women formed the second wave of feminism in the United States, France, and Mexico. In China, the role of women in the Cultural Revolution ensured their continued political participation. The 1960s proved to be a pivotal decade for women and global women's rights, and eventually led to the establishment, by the United Nations, of an "International Year of the Woman" conference, first held in Mexico City in 1975. Although this conference brought together politicians and women's rights advocates from all over the world, feminist groups organized demonstrations to demand action on those items that were not discussed at the conference; these issues included gay rights, violence against women, and environmental problems. At the fourth International Conference of Women, held in Beijing in 1995, many of the same demands made by activists in 1975 became key points of discussion. As of this writing in 2016, as candidates for the Republican presidential nomination continue to debate access to contraceptives and defunding Planned Parenthood, the feminist movement in the United States has been reignited by an issue that most thought was historical and widely settled—the legal right to choose an abortion. Meanwhile, the leading candidate for the Democratic nomination is Hillary Clinton, and another woman, Carly Fiorina, ran in the Republican primary race.

Today, as in 1968, the whole world is watching a series of watershed events unfold. In Tunisia, Libya, and Egypt, the political leaders supported by Western governments are failing to achieve any victories. In Egypt, the military gained power in the wake of Mubarak's collapse. When the military delayed elections, hundreds of thousands of Egyptians took to Tahrir Square to once again demand elections; when these elections were finally held, Islamist parties, such as the Muslim Brotherhood and Al Nour, combined to win 72 percent of the seats in the parliament. This overwhelming victory led to even greater instability in the region when Mohamed Morsi, the Muslim Brotherhood's candidate who was elected president in 2012, was ousted by General Abdel Fattah el-Sisi and his supporters. Today the ailing Hosni Mubarak is confined to a military hospital after having been convicted in May 2015 of corruption and awaits retrial on the charge of killing of Arab Spring protestors. Of course, overt protest is now forbidden by the al-Sisi government.

Libya is, by all metrics, a failed state split into two warring factions, as ever-growing chaos grips the land and its people. Yemen is also torn apart by civil war, a conflict into which neighboring Saudi Arabia has entered as an ally of the government of Abd Rabbuh Mansur Hadi (which the United States also supports from a distance), while Iran backs the opposing Houthi movement.

Of all of these civil conflicts in the Islamic world, the worst by far is in Syria. Following violent governmental repression of protests in the streets that were occasioned by the hopes raised by the Arab Spring, full-fledged civil war erupted in the summer of 2011. Five years later it rages on, having claimed probably more than 200,000 lives and displaced millions of people, with many of them seeking sanctuary outside of Syria's borders. The toll in human suffering in Syria cannot be calculated with any precision. The involvement to varying degrees of radical, supra-nationalistic Islamist forces, such as al-Qaeda and the so-called Islamic State, in these civil wars has only added to the overall anarchy and misery.

In 2016, the violence in chaos-enveloped Syria and Libya as well as fighting in Afghanistan and human-rights abuses in Egypt and Eritrea have occasioned a level of refugee-flight to areas of presumed sanctuary that has not been seen since the end of World War II. Countries from Turkey to Iceland struggle to handle this flood of misery- and fear-driven humanity, with Greece, Italy, and especially Germany bearing the brunt of the tide. The politicization of the humanitarian crisis continues as Republican presidential candidates debate whether refugees should be permitted to enter the United States because members of the Islamic State might have infiltrated the refugee population. The ISIS coordinated attacks in France in November 2015 furthered this fear, because one of the attackers allegedly had traveled to the West with refugees from Syria.

Western observers have characterized Tunisia as the sole successful state to emerge from the Arab Spring. In 2014, a parliament representing a broad spectrum of political ideologues and a secularist president were elected (although about 80 percent of young people between the ages of eighteen and twenty-five failed to vote), and in early 2015 a national unity government was formed. Yet attacks by jihadists have left over 120 dead and many more wounded since 2014, including large numbers of foreign tourists.

Democracy and reform have never been easy, and likewise those who led movements in 1968 did not emerge its political victors. In the wake of the strikes in Chicago and the Days of Rage, Americans elected Richard Nixon, a right-of-center Republican. In the presidential elections of 1970, Mexicans avoided the polls at numbers greater than previously, and the power of the PRI party remained intact. In France, Charles de Gaulle lost stature and power, but the Left that led the strike did not gain immediate power. Rather, the right-leaning Prime Minister George Pompidou was elected, followed by socialist François Mitterrand.

The Coming Spring or Winter?

The elections immediately following the 1968 protests seemed to affirm that the efforts of young people to change the world yielded few results. Yet those activists have had a profound, lasting impact on their nations. In the United States, many of the activists of 1968—including Bernardine Dohrn and her husband Bill Ayers—went on to careers in higher education. One of the founders of SDS, Tom Hayden, had a successful career in politics, and Gustin Reichbach, a leader in the protest movement at Columbia University, is today a Brooklyn Supreme Court Justice who still maintains his passion for social justice and leftist politics. France and Senegal have experienced similar outcomes. In Senegal, Mbaye Diack became Secretaire General adjoint de la presidence de la Republique (Deputy General Secretary to the President, similar to the White House Chief of Staff), and Michel Giraud, a Frenchman of Guadeloupean origin, is now a highly respected scholar who frequently appears on French television shows. In Mexico, leaders of the 1968 movement entered politics, the academy, and other public careers. In Czechoslovakia, Václav Havel, a leader of 1968, became the first president of the Czech Republic, and remained an influential global politician, intellectual, and scholar until his death in 2011.

Breaking with a tradition of silence, such high-ranking Chinese party members as Premier Wen Jiabao have begun to publicly discuss the brutality of the Cultural Revolution and how their families endured it. In Chile, Brazil, and Uruguay, leftist activists from the 1970s won in democratic presidential races. The Cuban Revolution, long a model for Latin American activists, has also evolved. Cuba and the United States worked to restore diplomatic ties beginning in 2014, and lifted travel bans and opened embassies in 2015. The activist Pope Francis also played a key role in reestablishing diplomatic relations. The regularizing of U.S.-Cuban diplomatic relations came decades after hostile relations. These developments in Latin America have changed much of the hemisphere.

Protests, demonstrations, and violent confrontations cause people to long for stability. Yet, as we have seen, the ongoing unrest in the Middle East has already changed, perhaps in lasting ways, the politics, economics, and societies of the region. In Europe, protests against austerity measures continue as politicians discuss the implementation of policies that will alter the social and economic lives of millions. In the United States, police forced Occupy Wall Street occupiers from their camps. In 2014 and 2015, police in various U.S. cities have been involved in attacks on unarmed civilians, and protests continue in other venues and cities, most notably Ferguson, Missouri; Baltimore, Maryland; Staten Island, New York; and Chicago, Illinois. As in 1968, the whole world is watching, but now those watching and participating are also texting, tweeting, and blogging about the events as they create history. The shifts in technology and how they have been harnessed in recent uprisings begs the question of whether today's social media would have made a difference in 1968. More significant to the moment, will the ability of activists to immediately voice and distribute their demands, criticism, images, and slogans ultimately lead to a more just and humane society once the strong men have been deposed? Or will dictators and radical ruling ideologues continue to replace previous authoritarian governments, despite the best attempts of protestors to promote democratic and humanitarian reforms?

FURTHER READING

Digitized Collections of U.S. Materials

With every passing decade, more studies and reflections on 1968 have entered the market. Study of the 1960s is reflected in college courses, bulletin boards (H-1960s), blogs, and journals (*The Sixties*).[1] Indeed, many university libraries host archival collections on the activism that took place during the 1960s. Some have exceedingly broad collections due to their location in key cities or states or due to protest leaders drawn from them or nearby institutions. Some collections more narrowly focus on the activism that took place on the campus. For example, the University Protest and Activism Collection, 1958–1999, at Columbia University consists of flyers, news clippings, transcripts, and images from the protests and can be accessed at http://www.columbia.edu/cu/lweb/archival/collections/ldpd_4080180/index.html. The forthcoming H. K. Yuen Social Movement Archive at the University of California at Berkeley documents activism of the 1960s and 70s in the Bay Area through a collection of audio files and primary evidence and is available at http://www.docspopuli.org/articles/Yuen.html. The History of 20th Century Protests and Social Action at the University of Wisconsin-Madison also contains images, clippings, and audio files on activism that took place on campus during the 1960s. See https://www.library.wisc.edu/archives/exhibits/campus-history-projects/protests-social-action-at-uw-madison-during-the-20th-century/. The Civil Rights Digital Library includes news broadcasts from local Georgia stations during the Civil Rights movement as well as other forms of primary evidence. It is located at http://crdl.usg.edu/. Finally, a number of original documents on Black student protests on U.S. campuses are available at San Francisco State and Cornell University: https://diva.sfsu.edu/collections/strike/2604 and http://guides.library.cornell.edu/content.php?pid=97406&sid=771201.

---

1. HNet (indicated here by "H-") is the Humanities Network that is composed of electronic bulletin boards.

Printed Primary Sources Relating to the U.S. Movements

For many years, former activists dominated the publishing of books and studies on the protest movements in the United States of the 1960s. Some of the most important eyewitness accounts in the United States include: Bill Ayers, *Fugitive Days: Memoirs of an Antiwar Activist* (Boston: Beacon Press, 2009); Todd Gitlin, *The Sixties: Days of Hope, Days of Rage* (New York: Bantam Books, 1993); Tom Hayden, *Rebel: A Personal History of the 1960s* (Pasadena: Red Hen Press, 2004); and Mark Rudd, *Underground: My Life with SDS and the Weathermen* (New York: Harper Collins, 2010). Along with male leaders, women activists have published their own recollections, including Jane Alpert, *Growing Up Underground* (New York: William Morrow, 1981) and Susan Stern, *With the Weathermen: The Personal Journey of a Revolutionary Woman* (New York: Doubleday, 1975).

Edited collections of interviews have also added to the growing body of literature, such as Ron Chepesiuk, *Sixties Radicals, Then and Now: Candid Conversations with Those Who Shaped the Era* (Jefferson, NC: McFarland, 1993). Document collections also provide a primary source history. Judith Albert Clavir and Stewart Edward, *The Sixties Papers: Documents of a Rebellious Decade* (New York: Praeger, 1984), contains writings from the early formation of SDS to the Black Power movement. Bernardine Dohrn and Bill Ayers, with Jeff Jones, have edited *Sing a Battle Song: The Revolutionary Poetry, Statements, and Communiqués of the Weather Underground, 1970–1974* (New York: Seven Stories Press, 2006).

China and the Cultural Revolution

Despite the importance of the Cultural Revolution in twentieth-century Chinese history, researching this period remains difficult. The subject is still taboo in China, and many archives are closed to those interested in the Cultural Revolution. And yet, despite this difficulty, what has been written about the Cultural Revolution provides tremendous insight into these ten years of struggle and turmoil.

There are three excellent introductions to the Cultural Revolution. Roderick MacFarquhar and Michael Schoenhals' *Mao's Last Revolution* (Cambridge, MA: Harvard University Press, 2006) provides perhaps the most detailed study of the entire Cultural Revolution. *Morning Sun,* a 2003 documentary by Carma Hinton, Geremie Barmé, and Richard Gordon and produced by Long Bow Village Films, is well made, and the interviews conducted by the filmmakers comprise an excellent collection of oral testimonials. Michael Schoenhals' *China's Cultural Revolution, 1966–1969: Not a Dinner Party* (Armonk, NY: M.E. Sharpe, 1996) offers a trove of primary sources from the Cultural Revolution, all translated into English.

Despite the enigmatic nature of the Cultural Revolution, Red Guards as well as their victims have published numerous accounts from this period. This "scar literature"—so named because of the sometimes horrific nature of the testimonials—first appeared in the 1980s, and represents an important outlet for those most deeply affected by the movement. For the perspective of a victim of the Cultural Revolution, see Yue Daiyun's *To the Storm: The Odyssey of a Revolutionary Chinese Woman* (Berkeley: University of California Press, 1987). Two excellent accounts from former Red Guards include Rae Yang's *Spider Eaters, a Memoir* (Berkley, CA: California University Press, 1997) and Gao Yuan's *Born Red: A Chronicle of the Cultural Revolution* (Stanford, CA: Stanford University Press, 1987). For a challenge to the monolithic narrative produced by "scar literature" see Arif Dirlik's essay "The Politics of the Cultural Revolution in Historical Perspective" in Kam Yee Law's *The Chinese Cultural Revolution Reconsidered: Beyond Purge and Holocaust* (New York: Palgrave Macmillan, 2003).

One question scholars have asked is why students broke into different factions during the Cultural Revolution. One scholar who has recently attempted to answer this question is Andrew Walder. His book *Fractured Rebellion: The Beijing Red Guard Movement* (Cambridge, MA: Harvard University Press, 2009) challenges the classic interpretation that students broke into factions based on family origins and class labels. Walder instead asserts that factionalism was much more complex and due to a variety of reasons, including individual experiences and political ideology.

Finally, various authors have offered fresh perspectives and new insight into specific aspects of the Cultural Revolution. Paul Clark's *The Chinese Cultural Revolution: A History* (New York: Cambridge University Press, 2008) examines the culture of the Cultural Revolution, discussing model operas, underground literature, and a variety of other facets of the movement. Yang Su's *Collective Killings in Rural China during the Cultural Revolution* (New York: Cambridge University Press, 2011) looks at mass violence that cost so many lives in the countryside during the Cultural

Revolution. Joseph Esherick, Paul G. Pickowicz, and Andrew Walder have edited a volume entitled *The Chinese Cultural Revolution as History* (Stanford, CA: Stanford University Press, 2006). The volume includes essays on students, violence, performance, and a variety of other topics. Finally, Jisen Ma's *The Cultural Revolution in the Foreign Ministry of China* (Hong Kong: Chinese University Press, 2004) examines events in the Foreign Ministry, which was temporarily occupied by radical students in 1967.

The Black Atlantic in 1968

Much has been written on African-American student movements during the sixties. Ella Baker, the civil rights activist, contributed to the growth of African-American student movements, as she led a series of meetings at Shaw University that eventually gave birth to the Student Nonviolent Coordinating Committee (SNCC) in 1960. Regarding her activities, see Barbara Ransby, *Ella Baker and the Black Freedom Movement: A Radical Democratic Vision* (Chapel Hill: University of North Carolina Press, 2003) and Joanne Grant, *Ella Baker: Freedom Bound* (New York: John Wiley, 1998). For relevant monographs on SNCC and its role in organizing the freedom rides, voters registration drives, and sit-in protests, see Wesley Hogan, *Many Minds, One Heart: SNCC's Dream for a New America* (Chapel Hill: University of North Carolina Press, 2007); Carson Clayborne, *In Struggle: SNCC and the Black Awakening of the 1960s* (Cambridge: Harvard University Press, 1981); and Faith Holsaert, Martha Noonan, Judy Richardson, Betty Garman Robinson, Jean Smith Young, and Dorothy M. Zellner, eds., *Hand on the Freedom Plow: Personal Accounts by Women in SNCC* (Urbana: University of Illinois Press, 2010).

By the late sixties, though landmark civil rights legislatures had been ratified, many African-American students felt as if nothing had changed. They grew more radical and joined the Black Power movement led by Stokely Carmichael, a former member of the Student Nonviolent Coordinating Committee (SNCC). For two excellent accounts of the Black Power movement, see William Van Deburg, *New Day in Babylon: The Black Power Movement and American Culture, 1965–1975* (Chicago: University of Chicago Press, 1992) and Jeffrey O. G. Ogbar, *Black Power: Radical Politics and African American Identity* (Baltimore: Johns Hopkins

University Press, 2004). Many African-American students also enlisted in the Black Panther party. See Jeffries Judson, Singh Nikhil, Pal Lewis, E. Melvin, and Steve McCutchen, eds., *The Black Panther Party Reconsidered* (New York: Black Classic Press, 1998).

Eventually, Black Power spilled into universities, a phenomenon that is well described in the following works. Fabio Rojas, *From Black Power to Black Studies: How a Radical Social Movement Became an Academic Discipline* (Baltimore: Johns Hopkins University Press, 2007); Stefan Bradley, *Harlem vs. Columbia University: Black Student Power in the Late 1960s* (Urbana: University of Illinois Press, 2009); and Alexander Downs, *Cornell '69: Liberalism and the Crisis of the American University* (Ithaca, NY: Cornell University Press, 1999).

France is another giant in the global historiography of May '68. The entire country was paralyzed during May and June 1968, when students and workers protested separately for improvements in the educational system and better labor conditions, respectively. There has been a deluge of studies analyzing the causes and legacy of May '68 in France. Much has been published in French, but there is also a strong body of literature in English. For instance, from a socio-economic perspective, Chris Howell explains how rapid modernization generated the protests in *Regulating Labor: The State and Industrial Relations Reform in Postwar France* (Princeton, NJ: Princeton University Press, 1992). Moreover, interdisciplinary scholars have demonstrate how "thirdworldism" (awareness of the plight of the Third World) and a desire for progressive cultural changes spurred the events. See Margaret Atack, *May '68 in French Fiction and Film: Rethinking Society, Rethinking Representation* (Oxford: Oxford University Press, 1999); Samantha Christiansen and Zachary A. Scarlett, eds., *The Third World in the Global 1960s* (New York: Berghan Books, 2013); Karen Dubinsky, Catherine Kroll, Susan Lord, Sean Mills, and Scott Rutherford, eds., *New World Coming: The Sixties and the Shaping of Global Consciousness* (Toronto: Between the Lines, 2009); and Kristin Ross, *May '68 and Its Afterlives* (Chicago: University of Chicago Press, 2002). Finally, for an interesting discussion linking social conflict in France with postcolonial migration (post-1960s) from the former French colonies and globalization, one should read Herman Lebovics, *Bringing the Empire Back Home: France in the Global Age* (Durham, NC: Duke University Press, 2004).

There were also protest movements in sub-Saharan Africa. From 1946 to 1959 African students and activists sought to end colonialism. In the former Francophone sub-Saharan African colonies there were a number of strikes, which paralyzed the colonial administration and spearheaded decolonization. For an excellent account of social unrest during that era, one may consult Frederick Cooper, *Decolonization and African Society: The Labor Question in French and British West Africa* (New York: Cambridge University Press, 1996); Frederick Cooper, *Africa Since 1940: The Past of the Present* (New York: Cambridge University Press, 2002); and Andrew Ivaska, *Cultured States: Youth, Gender, and Modern Style in 1960s Dar es Salaam* (Durham, NC: Duke University Press, 2011).

Eastern Europe in 1968

For a comparative analysis of the politics of 1968 throughout the Soviet bloc, see Paulina Bren, "1968 East and West: Visions of Political Change and Student Protest across the Iron Curtain," in Padraic Kenney and Gerd-Rainer Horn, eds., *Transnational Moments of Change: Europe 1945, 1968, 1989* (Lanham, MD: Rowan & Littlefield, 2004), 119–36. Timothy Ryback, *Rock Around the Bloc: A History of Rock Music in Eastern Europe and the Soviet Union* (New York: Oxford University Press, 1990) provides invaluable information about the formation of a Soviet bloc youth subculture and its links with global youth movements and music.

The Prague Spring has been the object of extensive attention in English-language works. As the face of Czechoslovak Communist reformism, Alexander Dubček has long fascinated writers and researchers. For his autobiography, see Alexander Dubček and Jiri Hochman, *Hope Dies Last: The Autobiography of Alexander Dubček* (New York: Kodansha, 1995), while William Shawcross' *Dubček: The First Full-Length Biography of the Leader Who Symbolized Freedom in Czechoslovakia* (New York: Touchstone Books, 1990) provides an accessible biography, published in the initial rush after the 1989 revolutions across Eastern Europe. The fall of Communism opened up to the public and researchers a wealth of previously unavailable archival resources. Jaromir Navratil edited *The Prague Spring 1968: A National Security Archive Documents Reader* (Budapest: Central European University Press, 1998), an invaluable collection of 140 documents focusing on elite-level politics in Czechoslovakia and the Warsaw Pact. Equally valuable are the digital archival collections of translated documents of the Cold War International History Project of the Woodrow Wilson Center in Washington, D.C., available through the Center's website, https://www.wilsoncenter.org.

Jiri Valenta, *Soviet Intervention in Czechoslovakia, 1968: Anatomy of a Decision* (Baltimore: Johns Hopkins University, 1991), is a scholarly analysis of the complex decision-making process that led to the invasion of Czechoslovakia. A more recent treatment of the invasion is provided by Gunter Bischof et al., eds., *The Prague Spring and the Warsaw Pact Invasion of Czechoslovakia in 1968* (Lanham, MD: Lexington Books, 2010). In Kieran Williams, *The Prague Spring and Its Aftermath: Czechoslovak Politics, 1968–1970* (Cambridge: Cambridge University Press, 1997), readers can find a well researched narrative that takes advantage of the sources available in post-Communist Czech and Slovak republics. Finally, Zdenek Mlynar and Mikhail Gorbachev, *Conversations with Gorbachev: On Perestroika, the Prague Spring, and the Crossroads of Socialism* (New York: Columbia University Press, 2002) provides insights into the long-term impact of the suppression of the Prague Spring from the perspectives of two influential Communist reformers.

Unlike the Prague Spring, the English-language historiography for Poland and Yugoslavia in 1968 is sparse. While the events associated with the birth of Solidarity in 1980 and the fall of the Communist government in 1989 have been adequately covered, there is no single book-length treatment of the March 1968 events in Poland. For a succinct overview, see Jerzy Eisler, "March 1968 in Poland," in Carole Fink, et al., eds., *1968: The World Transformed* (Cambridge: Cambridge University Press, 1998), 237–52. A very pertinent article on 1968 in the former Yugoslavia can be found in *Slavic Review*: Madigan Fichter, "Yugoslav Protest: Student Rebellion in Belgrade, Zagreb and Sarajevo in 1968," *Slavic Review* 75, no. 1 (Spring 2016): 99–121. Jacek Kuroń's and Karol Modzelewski's influential open letter to the Polish Communist Party that provided a Marxist critique of "bureaucratic socialism" has been translated in various editions and anthologies, including Kuroń and Modzelewski, *Solidarnosc: The Missing Link? A New Edition of Poland's Classic Socialist Revolutionary Manifesto* (London: Bookmarks, 1982). David Ost, *Solidarity and the Politics of Anti-Politics: Opposition and Reform in Poland Since 1968* (Philadelphia: Temple University Press, 1990) examines the links between the 1968 Polish radicals and the roots of the Solidarity movement of the 1980s. From the world of art and film, Andrzej Wajda's classic film *Man of Marble* (*Czlowiek z marmoru*, 1976), widely available with English subtitles, provides a fascinating cinematic treatment of the 1956, 1968, and

1970 protest movements in Poland, and the generational and class tensions between students and workers in the latter two years.

Of the three major Eastern European flashpoints in 1968, Yugoslavia has received the least attention in English-language historiography. An exception is Boris Kanzleiter's "Yugoslavia," in Martin Klimke and Joachim Scharloth, eds., *1968 in Europe: A History of Protest and Activism, 1956–1977* (New York: Palgrave Macmillan, 2008), 219–28. For a deeper study of the "Marxist humanist" intellectual movement that developed around the journal *Praxis*, see Gerson Sher, *Praxis: Marxist Criticism and Dissent in Socialist Yugoslavia* (Bloomington: Indiana University Press, 1977) as well as the translated documents available in Sher, ed., *Marxist Humanism and Praxis* (Buffalo, NY: Prometheus Books, 1978).

Mexico in 1968

As in the United States, Mexican activists produced the bulk of the initial literature on the 1968 Mexican student movement. Unfortunately, few of these memoirs have been translated into English. Elena Poniatowska's *Massacre in Mexico* (Columbia, MO: University of Missouri Press, 1991) contains translations of excerpts from a couple of memoirs as well as numerous eye-witness accounts.

In English, much of the work on Mexico 1968 focused on the Olympic Games and the protests of African-American athletes, particularly that of Tommie Smith and John Carlos. For a discussion of race and the Olympics, see Amy Bass, "Whose Broad Stripes and Bright Stars? Race, Nation, and Power at the 1968 Mexico City Olympics," in *Sports Matters: Race, Recreation, and Culture*, eds., John Bloom and Michael N. Willard (New York: New York University Press, 2002), 185–209, and her longer study, *Not the Triumph But the Struggle: The 1968 Olympics and the Black Athlete* (Minneapolis, MN: University of Minnesota Press, 2004). For an analysis of Mexico's attempts to host the games and the conflicts that emerged during the Olympics, see Kevin B. Witherspoon, *Before the Eyes of the World: Mexico and the 1968 Olympic Games* (DeKalb, IL: University of Northern Illinois Press, 2008).

Student protests long comprised the political culture of Mexico throughout the twentieth century, and there is a substantial historiography on Mexican social movements in Spanish. One of the earliest works to examine contemporary Mexican social movements is Judith Adler

Hellman, *Mexico in Crisis* (New York, Holmes & Meier, 1979). Other scholars have focused more narrowly on student protests, for example, Donald Mabry, *The Mexican University and the State: Student Conflicts, 1910–1971* (College Station: Texas A&M Press, 1982). For a general overview of the 1968 student movement see Elaine Carey, *Plaza of Sacrifices: Gender, Power, and Terror in 1968 Mexico* (Albuquerque: University of New Mexico Press, 2005). For another gender history approach, see Lessie Jo Frazier and Deborah Cohen, "Defining the Space of Mexico '68: Heroic Masculinity in the Prison and 'Women' in the Streets," *Hispanic American Historical Review* 83.4 (2003): 617–80. In *Refried Elvis: The Rise of the Mexican Counterculture* (Berkeley: University of California Press, 1999), Eric Zolov explores the Mexican counterculture that emerged in the 1960s. His more recent work examines the cultural implications of the Olympic Games on Mexican modernity: see "Showcasing the 'Land of Tomorrow': Mexico and the 1968 Olympics," *The Americas* 61.2 (2004): 159–88.

Over the past ten years, the scholarship on Mexico and the Cold War has grown. Recent scholarship has explored the long 1960s or the impact of student movements on Mexican politics and cultures, see Jaime Pensado, *Rebel Mexico: Student Unrest and Authoritarian Political Culture During the Long 1960s* (Redwood City, CA: Stanford University Press, 2013); Louise Walker, *Waking from the Dream: Mexico's Middle Classes after 1968* (Redwood City, CA: Stanford University Press, 2013); and Alex Aviña, *Specters of Revolution: Peasant Guerrilla in the Cold War Mexican Countryside* (New York: Oxford University Press, 2014).

In the years following the movement, certain journalists and newspapers played a key role in questioning the government's response post-1968: see Claire Brewster's "The Student Movement of 1968 and the Mexican Press: The Cases of *Excélsior* and *Siempre!*" in the *Bulletin of Latin American Research* 21.2 (2002): 171–90. Scholars and former activists of the Dirty War that followed are collected in Fernando Calderon and Adela Cedillo's *Challenging Authoritarianism in Mexico: Revolutionary Struggles and the "Dirty War"* (New York: Routledge, 2012). Museums, exhibitions, and art have continued to examine the movement. See Andrea Noble, "Recognizing Historical Injustice through Photography: Mexico 1968," *Theory, Culture, and Society* 27.7 (December 2010): 184–213, and Michelle Chase, "A Sonorous Review of '68: Review of the '68 Memorial in Mexico City," *The Sixties* 1.2 (2008): 223–27.

Latin America was a key battleground during the Cold War, and this topic has received greater attention in the past decade. For an overview of Latin America in the 1960s, see Diana Sorensen, *A Turbulent Decade Remembered: Scenes from the Latin American Sixties* (Stanford: Stanford University Press, 2007). Well worth reading are Jorge Castaneda, *Utopia Unarmed: The Latin American Left after the Cold War* (New York: Vintage, 1994); Gilbert Joseph and Daniela Spencer, *In from the Cold: Latin America's Encounter with the Cold War* (Durham, NC: Duke University Press, 2008); and Hal Brand, *Latin American's Cold War* (Cambridge, MA: Harvard University Press, 2010).

With the passage of time, more documents have become accessible. The National Security Archive contains numerous collections that examine the role of the United States in Latin America. For Mexico 1968, the archivists worked closely with Mexican journalists to produce an array of documentary projects. For documents on Latin America, Asia, and Europe, and the Middle East during the Cold War, see http://nsarchive.gwu.edu.

Placing the 1968 Protests into a Global Context

While biographies, eyewitness accounts, and learned monographs have added to our knowledge and insight regarding individual protest movements, a few books have appeared that position these movements as global and interconnected with one another, and that process began to happen in the late 1980s. Scholars have not only considered the international nature of the movements but also the rise and influence of the counterculture that spread across borders. Examples include: David Caute, *The Year of the Barricades: A Journey through 1968* (New York: Harper and Row, 1988); Robert Vincent Daniels, *Year of the Heroic Guerrilla: World Revolution and Counterrevolution in 1968* (New York: Basic Books, 1989); Carol Fink, Philipp Gassert, and Delef Junker, *1968: The World Transformed* (London: Cambridge University Press, 1998); and Mark Kurlansky, *1968: The Year That Rocked the World* (New York: Ballantine, 2004). Due to the complexity of the year and the numerous uprisings and events around the globe, each of these works contains interesting nuggets of information that might not be found in the other works. For younger historians, Michael T. Kaufman's *1968* (New York: Macmillian, 2009) introduces middle and high school enthusiasts to the era.

For excellent theoretical and regional approaches, the *American Historical Review* published a series of essays in February and April 2009. The scholars gathered in the collection offer interesting approaches to studying the counterculture, gender, and performance within the movements that spread from Japan to Germany to the United States. Also see Gerard J. Degroot, *Student Protests* (New York: Routledge, 2014) and the special issue "Latin America in the Global 1960s," *The Americas* 70:3 (January 2014).

Connecting 1968 to the Years That Followed

Many African nations have struggled with governance since gaining independence. Thus, most of the scholarship on protest in Africa is not only limited to the sixties, as scholars discuss a range of issues leading to poverty and social unrest. But if one wants to read excellent studies explaining why Africa is facing such challenges and what has been the Africans' reaction to a difficult transition, see Achilles Mbembe, *On the Postcolony* (Berkeley: University of California Press, 2001); Mahmood Mamdani, *Citizen and Subject: Contemporary Africa and the Legacy of Late Colonialism* (Princeton, NJ: Princeton University Press, 1996); and Michael Bratton and Nicolas Van de Wall, *Democratic Experiments in Africa: Regime Transitions in Comparative Perspective* (Cambridge: Cambridge University Press, 1998).

For connecting the 1968 movements to the events that took place in the late 1980s and early 1990s in Eastern Europe, see Paul Berman, *A Tale of Two Utopias: The Political Journeys of the Generation of 1968* (New York: W.W. Norton, 1996). For a more theoretical analysis see Jeremi Suri's *The Power and Protest: Global Revolution and the Rise of Détente* (Cambridge, MA: Harvard University Press, 2005). Jeremy Varon's *Bring the War Home: The Weather Underground, the Red Army Faction, and Revolutionary Violence in the Sixties and Seventies* (Berkley: University of California Press, 2004) takes a unique approach by comparing the U.S.-based and German-based militant groups that emerged from the 1960s.

Index

Civil Rights movement, U.S., xvii, xx,
    xxi–xxii, xxiv, xxix
    and Chinese social movements, 3, 26,
        31–32
    student role in, 47
    violence in, 33n
Cleaver, Eldridge, 23
Cold War, xvii, 4–5, 22, 61, 75
    and Latin America, 142
Columbia University, xiv, xxiii, xxiv, 48
Comité d'Action des Travailleurs et
        Etudiants des Territoires sous
        Domination Coloniale Française,
        41–42
Committee on Special Education Projects
        (COSEP), 49
Connor, "Bull," xix
Consejo Nacional de Huelga (CNH),
        96–98, 101, 102, 107, 108, 110
    posters, 114
Cornell University, 36, 49, 50, 52–53
    photos of, 54
Cuban Missile Crisis, 67
Cuban Revolution, xvii, 93, 96n, 131
Cueto Ramírez, Luis, 98, 114
Cultural Revolution, xvi, xxiii, 1, 131,
        134–35. *See also* Mao Zedong;
        People's Republic of China (PRC)
    and Civil Rights Movement, U.S.,
        31
    internationalism of, 19, 21, 23, 26
    mass rallies of, 28
    origins of, 2, 5–6
    vs. other social movements, 24
    outcomes of, 25
    promotion abroad, 18
    role of music in, 34, 35
    role of Vietnam War in, 21
    role of women in, 128
Czechoslovak Communist Party, 61, 71,
        73, 81, 87
Czechoslovakia, ix, xxix, xxviii, 1n, 83
    Communism in, 63, 72, 73, 78
    invasion of, 61, 62, 79–81, 89–90, 139
    leaders of, 68, 71, 131, 138
    normalization in, 82

photos of, 79
reforms in, 87
religious freedom in, 74
uprisings in, 125

Dakar University, 36, 44–46, 58–59
Days of Rage, ix, xxx
de Gaulle, Charles, 41, 68, 130
Democratic National Convention,
        Chicago, xxiii, xxvii, xxviii, xxx
Deng Xiaoping, vi, 4, 9, 11, 18
    handles student protestors, 26–27
Destroy the Four Olds campaign, 29
détente, 4–5
Detroit, Michigan, 33n
Díaz Ordaz, Gustavo, 68, 91
    and student protests, 98, 102, 105,
        109
Dohrn, Bernardine, xxvii, 131
Dubček, Alexander, 73, 74, 78, 79, 82
    cartoons, 90
    and Communist reform, 61, 62, 71,
        83, 90

East Berlin, 63, 64
East Germany, 61, 62, 63, 65, 78. *See also*
        Germany
    leaders of, 68
    normalization in, 81
    relationship with Czechoslovakia,
        79–80
    Soviet pressure of, 82
Eastern Europe, xvii, xxxii, 61, 74, 78,
        81
    activism in, 122, 125
    Communist Party in, 71
    Communist reform in, 64, 65, 73, 80
    leaders of, 68, 70
    patterns of protest across, 63
    protest music in, 124
    protests in, 62, 74, 83, 128, 140
    Soviet control of, x, xxxii
    successful revolution in, 82, 138
    youth protesters in, xvii, 72
Echeverría, Luis, 104, 105, 107, 110
    as president of Mexico, 111–12, 114